THE UNEXPECTED
BENEFITS
OF BEING
RUN OVER

THE UNEXPECTED BENEFITS OF BEING RUN OVER

NASEEM ROCHETTE

Misfit Blue

Published by Misfit Blue, South Orange, New Jersey
beautifullycrackedme.com

Cover design: Emily Weigel
Project management: Mari Kesselring
Editorial production: Abi Pollokoff
Image credits: Cover texture: Shutterstock/Valedi;
Cover author photograph: Yasmeen Anderson

ISBN (hardcover): 979-8-9872209-3-1
ISBN (paperback): 979-8-9872209-0-0
ISBN (ebook): 979-8-9872209-1-7
ISBN (audiobook): 979-8-9872209-2-4

Library of Congress Control Number: 2022923184

To Asha, Jasper, Kalyan, Westcott, Zahid, Robin, Maria, Lisa, Amy, Anjum, and my fluffies.

THANK YOU and THANK YOU AGAIN.
You help me in my darkest hours.
You fill my cracks with glitter and gold.
You give me the courage to share my story.
You help me be Unbreakable.

Unbreakable Day
[ˌənˈbrākəb(ə)l dā]
NOUN

The day that changes you and makes you realize how strong you are and reminds you how much you want to be alive.

A holiday to commemorate the joy of life, to honor the strength we find to navigate unimaginable moments, and to appreciate the people and community that help us pick up the pieces and make it through life's complexities.

CONTENTS

PREFACE

On May 21, 2018, I was hit by an SUV and run over three times. The car went forward, backward, and forward again, eventually stopping on top of me. While I was pinned underneath it, I had no doubt that I would die, that I'd leave my husband a widower, leave my three children without a mother. But here I am, years later, very much alive—yet changed. The person I was before the accident and the person I am now are different, with a new set of limitations and an altered worldview.

In those first very tough months, I made the decision that this accident would be a happy story. I decided to accept and even appreciate my changes, my cracks, as a part of my journey. On the first anniversary of the accident, my family and I decided to memorialize the day I almost died by remembering that I lived. We decided to call that day Unbreakable Day. It's our new holiday.

Now every year, on May 21, we celebrate Unbreakable Day. We celebrate the fact that I am here, that we are here together, and that I've learned a thing or two about life in the face of death and its aftermath, in a long and ongoing recovery.

I believe at some point everyone has an Unbreakable Day, or days. If you're alive, you've survived. No matter who you are or the particulars of what happened, you've been through something, and you did the best you could at the time. You continue to do the best you can. Every day gives you the opportunity to choose how to view your pain, and how to use that pain in transforming your life. I know that is easier said than done. So I am hoping that by sharing my journey with you and the things that I have learned, I can help you shape a story that makes you feel a little unbreakable too.

PART 1
IMPACT

CHAPTER 1

JUST STOP

New beginnings are often disguised as painful endings.

—Lao Tzu

I'm not overly concerned when the car first hits me. I'm annoyed but not worried. Stuff happens, and I am pretty sure I am OK.

It's a Honda Pilot, a midsize SUV, so the impact is at my waist, but I'm still standing. Well, standing and stunned. And growing a little bit angry. How dare she hit me!

I had been feeling so good. On top of the world actually. It was the most beautiful spring afternoon, the sky that perfect endless blue. I felt gorgeous, skinny, in command of work, grateful for my family, pleased with our new au pair. Then out of nowhere, this car.

I'm probably only standing there for a second or two, but time has frozen, as it sometimes does when you find yourself in the middle of a situation so far removed from your normal experience that you just can't process it and your brain needs extra time to catch up. A real-life freeze-frame. My mind is clear, expansive yet focused. My ego is big enough to be offended rather than scared as I register the car pressed up against my side.

This is ridiculous, I think. I can't believe a car just hit me!

A few more thoughts manage to pass through my mind in those couple of seconds. They are about as simple as you can get, shallow even.

Will I be black and blue? I wonder. Will we still be able to go out to dinner tonight?

And then, finally, At least this will be a great cocktail-party story!

Then the freeze-frame ends, and my cocktail-party thoughts are interrupted as time speeds up again. The driver accelerates. I fall forward onto the hood and then launch into the air and onto the roadway. Suddenly, everything is happening so fast, and yet my mind is completely blank. I can hear Wes, my husband, screaming, "Oh my god! That's my wife!"

Then, I'm on the ground, and the SUV is driving over me. The tires are going over my body. I hear screaming, my husband's voice but other voices too, and my own. I'm screaming.

"Stop!" I hear. "You hit someone!" and "You're driving over her!" and "Stop driving!" and "Just stop!" The voices have blended together into one panicked plea.

I'm being dragged up the hill. I don't know if it's five feet or fifty feet, only that there's tremendous pressure but no pain, and this terrible thudding sound, and I can't breathe. The car stops. Thank goodness, I think.

But then the car reverses. The tires pass over me again, over my legs, over my chest. There's a sharp burst of pain in my right knee. There's no time to linger on that sensation, because I'm being dragged, again, in the opposite direction, back down the hill. The weight above me, to the sides of me, seemingly everywhere, is so heavy. The ground is so hard, so rough and gritty. I hadn't realized how hard concrete really is before this moment. I wriggle around frantically, trying to free myself, to escape.

It dawns on me that something isn't right about this accident. It's going on too long. This should be over by now.

The car is moving forward again. This can't be happening. This is impossible. I hear Wes, desperation in his voice. He's shouting, "Stop! Just stop!"

He's so close and yet so far. I think of my kids, of Asha, Jasper, and Kaly. My beautiful babies. The loves of my life. My joie de vivre. I'll never see them again. Then I see the tires coming toward my head.

I'm going to die. I can tell from Wes's voice and from the cries of strangers. Time slows again. I have plenty of time to contemplate, to have a conversation with myself. In my mind, I'm alive, but also, I'm already dead. Somehow both are true.

I don't want to die. I love my kids so much. They need a mother; they need me. Wes lost his father when he was very young—I don't want to do that to my kids. No one could ever love them as much as I do. Do they know how much I love them? Do they know who I am, how I feel about things? Do they know what I would say to them in their special moments? Why didn't I write them letters so they would know? I should have written letters!

I answer my own questions, running through my memories, just like in the movies. I see our incredible vacations, to the Cayman Islands, to Costa Rica and Spain and Los Angeles and Belize. My children running along white-sand beaches, swimming in warm turquoise waters, sleeping in rooms with open windows that let in the scent of ocean and the sound of palm fronds clacking in the midnight breeze. My kids eating ice-cream cones—following our favorite rule: on vacation, ice cream is a vegetable and can be eaten at any time—vanilla and chocolate dripping off their chins. Sandy feet and sunburned noses, salt-tangled hair and gap teeth, the feeling of carrying a sleepy child who smells like sunshine. I see the five of us together late at night, eating burgers and pancakes in New York City diners, fresh off the airplane but not ready to go home, extending the fun just a little while longer.

Yes, I decide. Yes, they know how much I love them. They know who I am. We had adventures. We had fun. We had a great life.

I accept my fate.

The tire rolls over my head and neck.

I'm ready to let go.

I'm completely underneath the car, caged in by tires. I can see the muffler and other car parts, the brown-gray dust clinging to the undercarriage, and I can smell exhaust and rubber and metal. I can smell blood. I'm shocked back into the present. My world is four tires and the underside of a car and asphalt and pain. Claustrophobia tightens my chest, and for a moment I forget how to breathe.

I hear my husband's voice, begging, still shouting,

"Stop driving!" I hear the chorus of other voices, but Wes's rises above them all. His voice keeps me anchored. I'm so tired. I want to close my eyes, but, for some reason, I can't. Or maybe my eyes are already closed? I can't tell. I'm so confused.

More screaming. Finally, the car stops.

Am I alive? I wonder without emotion.

A car door opens; there's a woman's high-pitched screaming. There's no note of concern in it—only fear, or anguish, or simple distress. It's the kind of sound that draws attention to itself, that places itself, its needs, front and center. There are no words, no questions about the state of the person underneath the car.

My husband says, "Don't you even care what happened to her?"

Someone is trying to speak to me. I can't hear them; the driver's screaming is consuming my focus. "You need to move," someone says to her. "You need to be quiet. You need to leave." The screams fade.

A shadow leans down, a woman, whose features I can't distinguish. "What's your name?" she asks. "Do you know where you are?" Part of me knows that she is giving me busywork, trying to keep me conscious. I don't have the energy to answer. I just want to close my eyes and curl up in a ball. But I can't move. Not my head, not my body. The ground beneath my cheek feels rough. I can feel a wetness around my head, soaking into my hair. From the corner of my eye, I can see the pool expanding, red-black rivers running along the asphalt. I suspect my brain is bleeding, and that maybe my face has been ripped off. It feels so raw, gritty but not sandy—gritty and bumpy, like chunks are missing. I fear that my cheek is gone.

I am probably paralyzed. I recall from the movies that if you can wiggle your toes, then you're not paralyzed. I try and find that I can wiggle my fingers and toes. I'm filled with gratitude, followed shortly by terror. I can't move my arms or legs. Then the pain comes, like a tidal wave. There is so much pain, and it's everywhere.

Is this real? I wonder. This makes no sense.

I hear sirens in the distance, getting closer, and my husband speaking. His words don't register, only the tone, his fear and uncertainty.

"I can wiggle my fingers," I say. My voice is soft, scratchy; my throat is raw. "I'm not paralyzed. Can you grab my purse and my phone?"

"I have them," he says, relief in his voice. If I can care about my belongings, then I must not be too badly injured, right? I, too, am oddly comforted by the fact that my stuff is intact, and that my mind is intact enough to ask about them.

Doors open and slam. There are the sounds of still more voices, boots hitting the pavement, the squawking of radios. The faint thwack of a helicopter high above. Then there are scores of people around me. "Be still," they say. I see boots pacing, and faces, blurred by shadow, looking in. "Just be still for a little while longer. We need to get the car off you so we can move you."

I am still but impatient. I want to curl up in a ball and sleep. I want this to be over, but I am completely powerless. I am at the mercy of strangers.

To lift the car, they secure the tires with an inflatable wedge because the car is inclined up the hill. The last thing we need is for the car to roll over me again. I wait. I don't know how, but time simultaneously passes quickly and slowly, the reality of the present bleeding into memory. There's just so much pain.

I notice I have only one shoe on. One of my favorite shoes, my power heels, is gone. Ugh, I think, I lost a shoe. I love these shoes. It's so hard to find five-inch heels that you can walk around the city in. Then I notice my skirt is hiked up.

Oh my god, is my ass showing? Can the firemen see my ass? Can all of South Orange see my ass? What underwear am I wearing? Is it a cute pair?

Finally, the car is off me. I glimpse blue sky, green trees, worried faces. I breathe in fresh air. Someone is talking to me, but I can't make sense of what they're saying. Where's my husband? I want to ask but can't find the words.

Someone is holding my head in place; someone else is checking my pulse, their grip light on my wrist. "Can you squeeze my finger?" someone asks, and I think I do but am not sure. There are hands on my feet, and a stiff plastic collar is tightened around my neck. I panic for a second, but I can still breathe; it's OK. They are rolling me onto my side. A hand traces my spine; then I am on my back again, on a board. A strap goes over my chest and is tightened. There's a sharp pain, like a sparkler going off, and I gasp. A second strap. The sound of tape ripping, the sight of pads being placed alongside my ear in my peripheral vision—I can only see to the right. A strap across my hips, across my shins.

I am lifted away from the ground. The pain leaves a sliver for me to experience the lightness, the freedom.

"Excuse me," I say. "I need to know. Is my face ripped off?" I recognize my own vanity, feel guilty about asking, but I need to know. I also know there are probably more important things to worry about.

"Your face is not ripped off," one of the EMTs says. "Your face is fine."

Relief again courses through me, and I start to feel a bit more alert. Enough so that, when the ambulance driver tells a police officer that we are going to University Hospital in Newark, I have enough energy, or adrenaline, to debate.

"What about Summit or Morristown or Saint Barnabas in Livingston?" I ask. These hospitals are more . . . luxurious than Newark.

"Newark has the best Trauma," an EMT says.

"Do I need Trauma?" I ask.

"Yes," both EMTs respond simultaneously.

OK, Newark it is. Suddenly, I'm very hot. Like, boiling. "Are you hot?" I ask. "I'm really hot. I need to take off my jacket."

"Ma'am, please don't move. We'll need to cut it off."

"Cut it off? But it's my favorite!"

There's a pause. "Yes, ma'am." There's a hint of a smile in his voice. "We'll have to cut it off. It's kind of a mess anyway."

Oh gosh, I'm being so high maintenance, I think. Then again, I was just run over by a car, so maybe it's OK for me to be a little needy.

And why are they calling me ma'am? That makes me feel so old. . . . Did I forget to tell them my name?

A thought grabs me. Maybe this whole thing was my fault, my punishment for being too happy, for saying it out loud. And then the thought lets me go as the painkillers kick in.

PART 2
BEFORE

CHAPTER 2

THE JINX

I am in charge of how I feel, and today I am choosing happiness.

—Anonymous

I know it's ridiculous to think this was my fault. But you see, the day before the accident, I'd said out loud, "I'm happy." I jinxed myself.

The day had started off like any other weekend morning, with my husband, Westcott, and me juggling the hectic schedule of our family. As usual, we were dividing and conquering the barrage of soccer games, basketball practices, playdates, homework, dog walking, and errands that filled our weekend diaries. The routines were standard, but there was always one variable to negotiate: who drove with whom.

Having me as the driver was like pulling the short straw for my boys. Wes was the designated fun parent, the adult child who stopped for neon-colored Gatorades at 7-Eleven, took the kids out for celebratory (or consolatory) fast-food lunches after the games, or snuck in some little adventure before going back home. I usually didn't bother to compete in terms of fun—I had more "productive" things to do. That day, our nine-year-old son, Kalyan, was the lucky one getting a ride with his dad to his soccer game, while our eleven-year-old, Jasper, had to settle for me. Our thirteen-year-old daughter, Asha, was staying home to study.

I was feeling unusually light and unburdened, and I decided to surprise Jasper with a lunch out after his soccer game, just the two of us, for some overdue mother-son quality time. At a new Mexican restaurant in Millburn, we sat in the slightly tacky red pleather booth and ordered tacos and Jarritos. Cumbia played softly in the background, and limes and frying tortillas scented the air. I felt myself relax, eager to catch up with my intuitive and emotionally tuned-in child. Precocious in his desire for people around him to be happy, he likes to "fill buckets"; he pays close attention to other people's lives. He'd been well aware, maybe too aware, of my discontent the year before, when I was working with my older brother, Zahid, at a start-up.

Though my brother is eight years older than I am, he and I are very close, and we have strong mutual respect, both personally and professionally. We're in the same industry—enterprise technology—so going to work with him was a no-brainer when he asked me to be VP of sales. I didn't hesitate for a second, even though I loved my current job at an information technology company where I was running a large global team. I loved the people I worked with, this true dream team that somehow managed to get an incredible amount of work done while also having a great time. Once, over a working dinner, one of my reports asked, "Can we really write off this meal?"

"You do realize we're working?" I laughed. And we were. But we were also having so much fun that they had almost forgotten it was a working dinner.

I missed those days, but I was determined to support my brother in this important venture. Unfortunately, it became just too much. The pressure of launching a start-up, combined with being (1) the only executive team member not in California, (2) the only woman in a company of almost eighty men, and (3) the head of sales in an engineering company that was launching its first product, was intense, nearly suffocating. Oh, and (4) I was the CEO's little sister.

I felt that I needed to work extra hard so no one had reason to question me. I worried day and night that if I didn't succeed at running the sales team, Zahid would lose his job, or he wouldn't get the necessary funding, and it would be all my fault.

"That's what you get, Zahid," I could hear people saying in my nightmares, "for hiring your little sister."

Fear is certainly a good motivator, but is it the best motivator? Absolutely not. I was terrified of failure, of letting my brother down, and, at the same time, I felt the need to ignore my instincts and expertise because I didn't want to add to his stress levels. During debate or conflict, I accommodated rather than pushed back, a bad habit I'd thought I'd kicked. For so many years, I'd been working on speaking up and taking up space in a male-dominated field, and now I felt like I was backsliding. This, in turn, was giving me very uncomfortable flashbacks to my first job in San Francisco after graduate school.

It was 1996, and the Bay Area was the hippest place to be as it geared up for the dot-com boom. My cat and I had moved across the country from New Jersey, the ink on my Rutgers MBA still wet. I'd exchanged my glam Deadhead look—flowy linen, tie-dye shirts, fake fur—for nineties corporate skirt suits and blazers. I was twenty-five and determined to look professional, to be taken seriously in my new job. Not an easy feat in corporate America, where "boys were boys" and women kind of just had to deal with it.

Assertiveness training was still a thing—on top of our actual job, it was also our responsibility to learn to speak the corporate language, to act tough without being intimidating, to contribute without stepping on anyone's toes or bruising anyone's ego. I was careful. I couldn't control my coworkers or the culture at large, but I could control my own behavior. I didn't want to send the wrong message or get into a situation where a colleague hit on me and I'd have to turn them down and potentially face fallout. I didn't want to flirt, dammit; I wanted to work.

I finally said yes to happy hour about a month in. After a drink or two, a coworker blurted out, "You know, everyone at the office calls you 'the Ice Princess.'"

Yikes! No, I did not know that.

Apparently, my carefulness was read as aloofness, iciness, snobbishness. Shy men got to be mysterious or considered hyperfocused, while shy women, or women who may have had good reason to protect themselves, were labeled cold or mean. I realize now that this was completely sexist and unfair. But back then, I just wanted people to like me. Thankfully, I was smart enough to quit that job, leaving that toxic workplace behind but keeping the one good friend I'd made, Maria. Maria was like me: she looked good on paper—she was an uber high-achieving Stanford grad—but at her core, she was a misfit. We'd exchange looks across the room whenever our office started to seem like a frat house, a moment of solidarity that got me through the worst of it.

I'm glad to see how much corporate culture has changed over the last few decades. And my trouble at my brother's start-up in 2018 had zero to do with those kinds of issues. Still, I found myself reverting back to that shy person I'd been, often placating instead of advocating for myself and my expertise, just smoothing things over instead of standing up for what I knew to be true.

A couple of months in, Jasper had said, "Mom, you look so sad every time you come out of your office." I hadn't even realized that I was unhappy—that's how tuned in that kid is. He was absolutely right, and as soon as the company got funding, I left. "I just want to be your little sister again," I told Zahid.

Now, four months into my new job at Microsoft, Jasper wanted to know where my head was and confirm that his lighthearted, confident mom was back. He took a sip of his strawberry soda, then got straight to the point. "How's it going with the new job?" he asked. "Do you like it? Are you happy?"

See? I'm telling you; this guy is so tuned in.

I swallowed a cheesy bite of taco, then wiped a dab of hot sauce from my lower lip. "Honey, I love it," I said, feeling a smile spread across my face. It was true. Life just wasn't as heavy anymore. I'd started getting my mojo back a week into the new gig, and I was already making an impact with my clients. Few people would describe working at

Microsoft as low stress or low pressure, but for me, it felt like a cakewalk after what I'd been through.

And so I said it out loud: "I'm happy."

We spent the rest of lunch catching up on school, friends, sports, and summer plans, savoring our tacos and enjoying each other's company. Then we realized we needed to hustle if we were going to get to the many other things on our docket. Both Jasper and Kalyan were going to try out for the New York Red Bulls soccer camp. Before that, though, we had to welcome the new au pair from Brazil who was moving in with us that day.

That morning, I asked the kids to make welcome cards and put together a basket of treats for our au pair, and we planned to take her out for a fun family dinner that evening.

After lunch with Jasper, and once our au pair was fully welcomed and given the tour of the house, we left her to get settled while we took the boys to tryouts. Just before we walked out the door, I asked Asha to join us. She surprised me by saying yes, and she and I decided that, after we dropped off Wes and the boys, we would do a little shopping—one of our favorite mother-daughter activities.

It was close to four o'clock when we all headed out to my car, a blue Mini Cooper Clubman that Wes and I had recently purchased. Whenever we were out together, Westcott instinctively got behind the wheel—although it was usually the wheel of the big family car, a Mazda CX9. This was "my" car, and he didn't drive it often enough to remember that it sits low to the ground and runs on high-performance tires, which means it can't handle potholes. About one hundred yards into our journey—less than two blocks from home—we hit a small but deep pothole with a jolt and a thud. The low-air-pressure light immediately flashed. Wes pulled over to confirm that, yes, the front tire was flat.

We quickly drove home, the flat tire making that ominous "kathunk, kathunk" sound the entire way, and loaded up in the much roomier Mazda to restart our trip. (You'll find this little mishap becomes important to the story later on!)

Luckily, we got to the tryouts just in time, as both Kaly and Jasper hate to be late. It stresses them out, which then stresses me out as it's often my fault. Between work, the kids, daily exercise, and regular dinners out, I lead a "just in time" life, which for them meant I was always trying to fit in just one more errand or work call before we got out the door.

Once we arrived, Asha and I dropped Wes and the boys and, as planned, went to grab an hour of shopping before we had to return to pick them up. After we had spent about thirty minutes browsing, Wes called.

"Jasper's hurt his arm," he said. "You need to get back here."

I looked down at the couple of shirts and the pair of pants draped over my arm. I can rarely pass up a good bargain, but waiting in line to make the purchase seemed irresponsible. Asha and I handed our finds to a salesclerk and beelined it to the car.

My heart was racing as I drove. Not only is Wes the fun parent; he's also the chill parent, which means that I can't always tell the level of seriousness (based on my less-chill rubric of seriousness) of a situation by the way he talks about it. But my husband wouldn't have called if the injury hadn't sidelined our son, and I knew Jasper would be bummed about getting hurt in the middle of spring sports season.

The field lot was packed with SUVs, American trucks, Japanese sedans, and soccer-mom minivans. As I pulled in, the security guy rushed over. "Ma'am," he said, "the lot is full. You're going to have to park somewhere else."

"My son's injured," I said, barely slowing down. I made my own parking spot and ran toward the bleachers, Asha right behind me. I have no poker face, so my panic must have been apparent. Just before I reached the field, someone called out, "You must be the boy's mom. Your son's OK. He's over there with your husband."

I wound my way through the crowd and finally reached the bleachers, where I found Jasper sitting calmly. "Hi, Mom," he said, and smiled. Wes had brought him a soda and candy bar from the vending machine, and Jasper was icing his arm while they waited for Kaly to finish.

"Where does it hurt?" I asked. "What's your pain level? Do you think it's broken?" I'm sure you've seen other moms like this, slightly overreacting yet rightly concerned. I was ready to drop everything and get Jasper out of there, but Wes, as usual, was even tempered about it. His calm provides a wonderful balance to my ever-present and pressing need for action. And apparently, he felt this was urgent enough for Asha and me to stop shopping but not urgent enough for us to pull Kaly off the field. Anyway, Jasper wanted to wait to talk to the head coach.

When tryouts were over, we spoke to the coach and were relieved to hear that he had seen Jasper play long enough to secure a spot at camp—both boys would be accepted. Thank goodness! That would make the next few weeks of missed games more bearable.

"But you should probably get to the emergency room," he added.

That was not what we usually did. Our accident MO was to call my dad, who was a doctor, a hematologist-oncologist, or to stop by to see our friend Ethan, an ER pediatrician. But we followed the coach's suggestion and drove straight to the hospital. Wes dropped me and Jasper off, all of us hoping that it would just be a quick stop. When we realized we were in for an hour-or-two wait, the whole gang (Wes, Kaly, and Asha) joined us, and we let our new au pair know that we couldn't take her out for dinner that night. I felt so bad about disappointing her and promised we would do something fun the next evening.

We had our own private triage room. The four of us kept Jasper company while he waited for X-rays, saw the doctor, and then got his broken arm wrapped up in a supportive sling until he could get a cast fitted. I don't remember what we talked about during that hour, just that we had so much fun hanging out. It was an oddly enjoyable moment together—our first family adventure in the ER.

We finally got home that night around nine o'clock. I was a little stressed about getting everyone settled so that I would have a moment to myself to prepare for an important meeting the next day. Wes, knowing how much I wanted to be on my game, offered to change our Monday plan. I work from home often and almost every Monday, so normally I would handle whatever mad juggle was needed. But with our two unexpected complications, namely the flat tire and the broken arm, Wes offered to handle everything—getting my flat fixed, training the au pair, and taking Jasper to the doctor for the cast. Wes rarely worked from home—remember, this was 2018—so it was a noticeable kindness and huge help to me, although I think he also felt some guilt for driving over that pothole. This was also the first time in thirteen years of childcare that I wasn't training our sitter on their first day on the job, but I knew Wes could handle it, so I accepted his generous offer. I'd kill it at the meeting, get home early, and take the family out for that special welcome dinner. I had it all figured out and under control.

CHAPTER 3

A BEAUTIFUL
SPRING DAY

When you arise in the morning, think of
what a precious privilege it is to be alive—
to breathe, to think, to enjoy, to love.
—Marcus Aurelius

I checked the weather on my phone first thing the next
morning—it was going to be warm and sunny, with a high
in the mid-seventies. Perfect. Then I jumped on the scale,
as I do every morning, and, like the weather forecast, it
was kind. I was at my ideal "skinny" weight of ninety-eight
pounds, the payoff of all my hours on the Peloton cycle and
in kickboxing classes, all my hard work to stay double dig-
its. I know, I know; you can tell me that I was behind the
times, that we don't put so much emphasis on weight anymore, that we should love our bodies no matter the size.
But I'm a product of my generation, OK?

I rode eleven miles in forty-five minutes on my Peloton, then took a shower. Standing before my closet in my white fluffy bathrobe, I looked at my wardrobe. Obviously, it was a day for a skinny outfit and big-power heels. I can't explain why, but high heels give me a confidence boost. Maybe I stand up straighter or just feel more dressed up, but whatever the case, I never go to an important meeting in flats. I also tend toward some variation of an all-black ensemble: black pants, black leggings, black dresses or, on a skinny day like that day, a tight black skirt. That morning I paired my Diane von Furstenberg high-waisted skirt with a plain black T-shirt and, to throw in a little color, my favorite denim jacket, a light blue short fitted jacket with extra-tight sleeves. It was slightly constricting, but it made my arms look skinny, so it was worth the discomfort. I put some blingy rings on, like I always do, and checked my favorite diamond studs with secure lock backs that never leave my ears. To top it off, or to bottom it off, I slid my feet into five-inch Stuart Weitzman wedge platform sandals, which are surprisingly comfortable and would give me that boost while I walked around the city.

This version of me—this confident go-getter in five-inch heels—was a far cry from who I'd been as an Indian Muslim girl growing up in the suburbs of New Jersey in the seventies and eighties. My family was one of a handful of Indian families in town, and it didn't help matters any that our last name, Hussain, just so happened to sound like that of a despot in the Middle East. From the moment I stepped foot in my kindergarten classroom, I knew how different I was from the other kids, who were white and Christian or white and Jewish. Not brown. Not Muslim. Not the daughter of

Indian immigrants. Even though my dad's professional sta-
tus as a hematologist-oncologist gave my family a leg up,
we were very obviously different.

I hated being different.

Being different made me shy and afraid. On top of
that, my father was very protective, and probably struggling with his own sense of differentness and desire to
belong (though of course I didn't know that at the time).
Perhaps, too, it was a by-product of the job—he saw sick-
ness and death every day, and even with his training and
experience and the best, newest treatments, there was so
much he couldn't control. He was a warm, friendly, caring
person, and he got close to patients, some of whom got
sicker, some of whom died. My dad left his pain at the office, but it's impossible to lose patients and not be affected.
Underneath his jovial spirit ran a taut string of anxiety; he
couldn't bear for me to be in danger, even the kind that is
part of an American childhood, like learning to ride a bike
or swim. He worried constantly over things that wouldn't
faze other parents, especially white American-born parents in that shag-carpeted, latchkey, laissez-faire era. For
my dad, a skinned knee was enough to cause panic and
demand I stop running when I played outside.

For most kids, there's no distinct point where their parents' issues stop and their sense of self begins. I was no
exception. I didn't know that my dad didn't want me to try
new things because he was afraid; instead, I felt like there
was something wrong with me, that I was destined to fail.
So I never even tried. Not sports, not acting, not music. I
just sat on the sidelines and watched.

The weird thing is, my mom was a gambler. I mean
that literally. She'd taught herself to be a stockbroker, and

every week she'd go to Atlantic City to play poker with a couple of guys she worked with. Where my dad was cautious, she was spontaneous, taking me on impromptu shopping trips when my dad was working late or away at conferences (a mother-daughter tradition I've continued with Asha). My mom loved to dress up in beautiful, brightly colored saris and decadent jewelry for get-togethers with our Indian community on weekends. By white American standards, my parents were fairly conservative, but they were essentially the Beyoncé and Jay-Z of our small Indian community, and when they were with their friends, they sure could party. Almost every weekend they'd give us a spoonful of purple children's Dimetapp so we'd fall asleep early, and they could imbibe and do their thing. (No judgment here—I thought it was delicious, and I still envy my parents' amazing social life!)

During the week, my mom wore stylish Western clothes, the eighties' version of the power outfit: skirt suits that were the height of business-lady fashion in teal and brick red, with shoulder pads and beige pantyhose in pointy-heeled shoes that always looked chic and very painful. Her dark hair was short, in a side-swept bob with lots of volume on top. From her, I learned to love fashion, and in her, I got to see the rare example of a vibrant woman who was both a professional and a mother in our New Jersey suburb.

That said, she made a few questionable decisions with my clothes. The thought of a pair of red-checkered pants I wore in first grade still makes me shudder, even if it was the coolest pair of red-checkered pants available at the time. It was cruel to make me wear them—I was shy and quiet, and these pants were screaming. I even tried to hide them in the linen closet. She found them and didn't take the hint, so I was forced to wear them at least a dozen more times. (Hey, I think I just figured out why I never wear red!)

When I got older, I spent weekends picking out my own clothes, shopping for high-rise jeans (which are back in style, thank you very much) and oversized blazers at the Limited and Macy's in the mall. Even though I won "Best Dressed" in middle school, I always felt insecure. I think my focus on clothes (and weight) was something that I could control, a way of fitting in more. Still, a fabulous outfit didn't take away the little things that reminded me that I was different—the assumption that I would go to the sixth-grade dance with the new boy in school because he was Indian, or being the only one in the class to not get invited to my close friend's bar mitzvah because his parents "didn't think you'd want to come." Why wouldn't I have wanted to come?

It was never overt. No one ever called me a bad name or made an explicitly racist comment meant to hurt or be-little me. This made the underlying attitude difficult to see, especially as a kid, and made my sense of not belonging more confusing.

Am I just being oversensitive? I'd wonder.

I wasn't bullied, and I did well in school, didn't I? What was the problem? I assumed it must have been me.

In the afternoons, from third grade on, I'd get home and call my mom at work first thing to let her know I was safe and sound. I would do my daily chores—wipe down the kitchen and bathroom counters, collect the garbage, put the breakfast dishes away—and then meet up with my friends for the rest of the afternoon. Normal stuff, right? Yet I always felt out of place, and to make it worse, I knew, for a fact, that no one thought I was pretty. I was a girl; it was the eighties, and that was on the top of my list of aspirations. Anyway, we all want to be considered attractive, don't we?

Then, in the tenth grade, a boy liked me for the first time. Let's call this boy Gary. Gary was white and tall and fit, with a gorgeous flop of blond hair that he periodically swept out of his big blue eyes. I'd had a crush on him for months by the time he asked me out. By spring, we were spending every free minute together. He got me. He really got me. Finally, someone appreciated me even though I was different.

One summer night, we were hanging out with friends down at the Jersey Shore, on the eighteen-mile strip of sand that makes up Long Beach Island. The late-night bonfire cast a warm glow on our young faces, and sparks crackled in the balmy air. Gary was sitting next to me on an old log, his big hand holding my small one. He leaned in. "Let's go for a drive," he whispered in my ear. I shivered, then followed him up the beach to his parents' old wood-paneled station wagon. We drove a little way down Long Beach Boulevard and parked in a quiet spot, the back of the hatch facing the ocean.

We climbed in the back of the car, our bare feet exposed to the light sea breeze, the stars brilliant above the haze of city lights. Inside, it was cozy and private and pure romance. We talked and laughed and kissed a little, him gazing at me with those earnest blue eyes.

"You know," he said, brushing away a strand of hair that had gotten stuck to my pink lip gloss, "every guy would think you are so beautiful if you were white."

Record scratch. Say what? Thing was, he genuinely thought that he was giving me a compliment. Truly, he did.

He was a beautiful white boy in a tony white town in 1986—
he didn't know any better. No one did. Well, I did, at least
a little bit. Maybe he didn't get me as much as I thought
he did.

My self-confidence took a long hiatus after that. If I
could go back, I would tell my teenage self that Gary was
an idiot. Even if he had no idea of what he was saying and
didn't mean harm, he had caused harm. He had said one
of my unarticulated fears out loud, expecting me to swoon.
I did not swoon. Instead, I froze. I said nothing, and then
pretended like it had never happened.

Despite this gut punch to my budding self-esteem, I
still had hope that life after high school would be better,
that I could reinvent myself into someone cooler and more
confident. Maybe, then, I'd belong, once I had the right
hairstyle and the right references and the right skin color.
. . . Well, some things you just can't change.

Thank goodness for my dear friend Lisa, who imparted
some wisdom just before we went our separate ways after
graduation. We were sitting on my deck next to the pool
that my dad was too afraid to let me learn to swim in.

My parents were out, as usual, and we had the place
to ourselves. She looked me in the eye, slightly tilted her
head, and with a straight face she said, "If we get to college, and we don't like who we are, why would anyone else
like us?"

I don't think she realized what a profound statement
that was, as we both just kind of nodded and went back to
a more usual topic, like what was happening on General
Hospital—the soap opera we had both been watching and
discussing since elementary school. That idea flipped a
switch for me, though.

• ♦ •

Gary might not have recognized me more than twenty years later, on that perfect May day in 2018. Whether or not I was beautiful by the narrow definition of a sheltered boy in 1986, or by anyone's standards of beauty, I *felt* beautiful and confident in my skinny skirt and five-inch heels. I was ready to conquer my workday. Even the nuisance of the flat tire didn't put a stutter in my step, especially since Wes had kindly offered to take over kid-drop-off duties, after delivering me to the South Orange train station. "Text or call me when you're on your way back," he said as I got out of the car. "I'll be here to pick you up."

I worked during the half-hour train ride to Penn Station, then caught the subway downtown, disembarking near my client's office in the Financial District. I'd already done the heavy lifting on this project, and so I was somewhat relaxed as I took the elevator to the top floor. The client met me at the reception desk and, all smiles, led me to the conference room, where floor-to-ceiling windows revealed the cloudless sky doming a gray Hudson, a proud Lady Liberty, and the sprawl of New Jersey beyond. The meeting went flawlessly. Everyone was delighted, and even their CEO came out to thank me.

That felt good. Really good.

I had only been working with them for a couple of months, so it was particularly gratifying to have made an impact so quickly. My new boss was over the moon.

Around three o'clock, when the meeting wound down, a colleague and I walked out of the building together. Normally, I would have gone with him back to our office in Midtown, but I had a kid with a broken arm and a brand-new au pair at home. "Hey," I said, putting on my

sunglasses. "I'm going to head out. I'll jump on that conference call in"—I checked my phone for the time—"twenty
minutes." I was juggling, but I was doing it well.

I walked to the subway station, feeling on top of the
world, the honking horns and jostling pedestrians and "eau
de garbage" (you know the one) a pleasant urban buzz in
my consciousness. My conversation with Jasper the day
before had brought some painful memories of the previous year to the surface, but with this brand-new success
under my belt, I could look at them from a better vantage
point, with a little more emotional distance. Now I felt like
my adult self, the person who had worked hard and built
something great. The person who had earned the right to
smile with pride and feel fabulous in five-inch power heels.

I hopped on the train back uptown and got off at Penn
Station to catch the 3:20 p.m. train to South Orange, timing it so I would be on the New Jersey side of the tunnel for
my 3:30 p.m. call. As always, I took a seat near the window
and looked out as I listened in. My mind was in an open,
relaxed state as we passed alongside the northern New
Jersey skylines. A bird or two zooming past over marshy
shores, the Red Bulls soccer stadium and strip malls and
industrial complexes. It was a familiar ride, and I didn't really see what I was looking at until the announcement of our
arrival at Brick Church station. I was almost home. Little
did I know that this would be the last peaceful commute in
a very long time.

My call continued as the train took a turn to the south-
west. By the time I reached my stop, South Orange, it was
around four o'clock. Wes had been expecting me to let him
know before I reached the station so he could be there to
pick me up, but I was still on the conference call as I walked

out into the late-afternoon sunshine. Anyway, I wanted a few more minutes to myself to revel in the glory of the day, to enjoy a slow moment before our evening plans unfurled. Unlike most days when I drove and headed to the parking lot, I walked out the front of the train station into downtown South Orange. A Starbucks or maybe an ice cream called to me, but then I came to my senses and remembered I was feeling skinny. Plus we were going out for dinner, and I didn't want to ruin my appetite.

I passed a posse of middle schoolers whom I'd known since they were cuddly little toddlers but didn't see Asha in the mix. It was lovely to watch the kids grow up together. I knew better than to cramp their style, so I just said a quick hello and kept walking. That's when I finally called Wes.

"Why didn't you call me earlier?" he asked. "I would have come down to wait for you."

He was excited to tell me about his day—the tire, Jasper's cast, the au pair. But it was too gorgeous to chat on the phone, so I said, "Meet me halfway and tell me when I see you."

Meeting Wes halfway would mean I could continue to enjoy a short walk, yet I would be spared from walking up the hill in my five-inch heels that, though comfortable, weren't that comfortable.

About midway, I saw my husband pulled over at the stop sign across the street from South Orange Middle School. He was in an unfamiliar Mini Cooper, a brown loaner car. I was standing in front of the school, at the bottom of a "T" intersection made up of Ridgewood Road and Tillou Road. Ridgewood is not a main arterial, but it is highly traveled. Tillou Road has a slight curve before it goes straight uphill, and it's a long tree-lined street with stately hundred-year-old Tudors and Colonials with large front lawns, and gaslights along the sidewalks. It is one of Wes's favorite streets and the one he always takes to get to or from home to downtown South Orange.

He saw me right after I saw him and yelled, "Nas!" in his loud, deep voice that easily carries over crowded rooms, makes everyone's head turn, and thoroughly embarrasses our kids on a regular basis. Occasionally it embarrasses me, too, although usually that's trumped by the joy I feel when I see my lighthearted husband. Wes is one of those rare people with a natural enthusiasm for life. Early on in our relationship, he'd say, "Sleep is for the weak" and keep us out all night with friends or on impromptu road trips or at clubs and concerts. I like to believe I share Westcott's enthusiasm for life, just not in the same loud, sleep-deprived way.

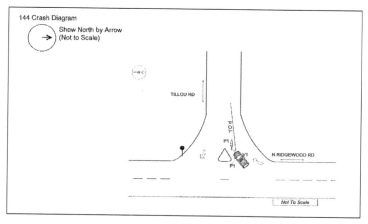

Figure 1. SEQ Figure * ARABIC 2: Drawing of Intersection from Police Report

South Orange Middle School gets out at 3:10 p.m., so by 4:00 p.m., the kids were gone, and it was relatively quiet, though there were a few people walking dogs, going about their day, and a preschooler selling lemonade just up the hill on Tillou. Even though it wasn't crowded, I didn't yell back (and draw further attention to myself), so I held up a pointer finger to signal one minute. I had my sunglasses on, but I could clearly see him look at me, acknowledge my signal, and turn back to his iPhone to read while he waited. (Wes is a walking encyclopedia and is always reading something or checking sports scores.)

As he was parked catty-corner from me and the road was empty, I could have easily just run over to him. I didn't want to jaywalk, though; even if no kids were around, it would have just felt . . . wrong. Or rude. It's not like I was in a big rush, and crosswalks were invented for a reason (another detail that would later prove to be important to note).

I crossed Ridgewood Road first, then entered the second crosswalk on Tillou. I was in the middle of the road when I saw a white SUV coming toward me. I was already in the crosswalk, so I yelled "Hey!" in a loud, commanding voice, the kind of voice I can usually only muster when there is a vicious man-eating raccoon rooting around in the trash.

That "Hey!" startled Wes, who looked up from his phone. I think it must have also startled the driver, because she paused, and I had enough time to slam my hand down on the hood of her car. I remember slamming it down with real force. I remember the sound it made on impact. The SUV stopped. I was still standing—but only for a very long second.

PART 3
AFTER

CHAPTER

BROKEN

You never know how strong you are until
being strong is the only choice you have.
—Bob Marley

When my long second was over and the driver had finished
driving over me (and over, and over), I found myself stuck
underneath the car. It was an unforgettable eternity lying
there. Stuck. Powerless. Exhausted. Waiting.

First waiting to die and then, when that didn't happen,
waiting for the first responders to get the car off me and
load me into the ambulance. Time slowed and sped up;
memory merged with the present; searing pain replaced
numbness and shock. Blood pooled around me on the
pavement. I desperately missed my kids, and I knew their
nightmare was just beginning.

Wes would have to handle that too. Seeing his wife almost die may have been the easier part.

• ◆ •

Wes followed the ambulance in the loaner Mini Cooper. This was the au pair's very first day; we barely knew her, and there was no way he could call her with this kind of news. So he called Asha. The conversation was short.

"Hey, Dad," Asha said. "What's up?"

Wes cleared his throat. Can you imagine how difficult these words would be to say? For my daughter to hear? "Asha, Mom was in an accident. She . . . she was run over by a car."

Asha was quiet for a moment. "Is it bad?"

"Yes." Then he must have realized that he was talking to a thirteen-year-old about her mother. He probably didn't want to downplay it—he'd seen the car drive over my neck, and he knew it was possible that I was paralyzed—but he also didn't want to scare her. "But we don't know the extent of her injuries. We just don't know, OK?"

Another pause. "What should I tell Jasper and Kaly?"

"Just tell them there was an accident. But wait until I call you from the hospital."

Asha held on to that information for fifteen minutes while she waited for her dad to call back. Wes, meanwhile, had made it to the hospital, where he was pacing in the waiting room. The nurses wouldn't let him in to see me, and they didn't have updates on what was happening or an idea of when he could go in. He called Asha again.

"I'm here at Newark," he said. "Nothing new to report. Can you tell your brothers now? And do you think you'll be able to help the au pair get you here? She doesn't know the area at all. I'll call again as soon as I know anything."

"Yes, Dad," she said. Then she went outside, where the

au pair was playing basketball with her brothers. "Mom's been in an accident," Asha told them. Jasper, in his new cast, let the basketball roll away down the driveway.

"You're joking," Kaly said, laughing. Asha shook her head. His smile fell away. "You're joking, right?"

"She's at the hospital. Dad's there. He wants us to meet him." She turned toward the au pair. "Can you drive us?"

While Asha was delivering this news and then directing the au pair around Newark using Google Maps, Wes was making phone calls. First, he called my brother, who immediately booked a ticket from San Francisco to Newark. "Call our parents," Zahid told Wes, who was avoiding the inevitable because we don't like to worry them—their default setting is already worried, set to high, and he didn't want to freak them out. "Wes, our dad is a doctor," Zahid reminded him. "He's usually pretty calm in these situations."

So Wes called my dad. Again he had to summon the courage to say the unthinkable. "Shafkat," he said, when my dad picked up, "Nas was in an accident."

Wes then explained the situation, my dad asking questions to which my husband didn't have any answers. My dad didn't freak out. In these kinds of crises, he was able to take off his parent hat and put on his unemotional white lab coat, to set his feelings aside in order to assess the situation. My parents made the hard decision that my mother would stay behind; she suffered from Parkinson's and rheumatoid arthritis, and making the hour-long drive from South Jersey to the hospital would be an ordeal and use up valuable time. "Go," she told my dad.

"OK," my dad said to Wes. "I'm on my way."

He arrived an hour later to find Wes still pacing,

wearing a groove into the threadbare waiting-room carpet. The kids had arrived and were sitting silently, their faces frozen. "They won't let me in," Wes said.

My dad, the seasoned doctor, was in his element. "I'll see what I can do," he said.

But even with his doctor's confidence, his familiarity with the sights and sounds and rituals of the setting, my dad couldn't extract any more information. Finally, after what must have felt like a lifetime, a nurse entered the waiting room. "She's alive," she said. "It's a miracle."

The ambulance had delivered me to a crowded room full of doctors and nurses. I was lucid enough to describe what had happened, and to register the gasps of disbelief among these medical providers who had seen everything: gun violence, motorcycle accidents, stabbings, overdoses. Still, they gasped when I told them that I had been run over three times. "What do you mean, 'three times'?" they'd ask, and I'd explain it all over again. The SUV drove forward, then backed up, then drove forward again, I'd explain. The tires went over me five times. Saying it out loud did not make sense of it.

There followed an exhale or a raising of eyebrows or both.

My memory of the ER is blurry. I remember the pain. I remember the team taking off my jewelry, my wedding ring, and some other special and sentimental pieces that I really didn't want removed.

"Can I hold on to the bag of jewelry during the X-rays?" I asked, knowing how ridiculous I sounded. That was met with a chuckle and some assurance that it would be safe in the room. From the second and third ear piercings in my left ear and the second piercing in my right ear, they removed my tiny diamond studs. These had secure posts designed to keep them on all the time, and one nurse had to hold my head and neck still while a couple of others tried to twist them off. It was very uncomfortable, and they broke two in their attempt. I was getting frustrated and impatient—this prodding was surprisingly painful, too much to tolerate on top of all the other issues. For the first time since the ordeal began, I started to cry. This was the last straw.

Finally, I said, "Just let me do it," and painfully, tearfully, worked the last earring off. No idea how I mustered the strength or even had the mobility to lift my arm.

My eyes were closed most of the time. I just couldn't bear the light. Also, disconcertingly, one of my eyes seemed to be stuck shut. Voices floated above me, talking about me, and gurney wheels squeaked on the linoleum as I was wheeled into various rooms for various exams. Beyond the scent of my own blood was the smell of rubbing alcohol, latex, ammonia, chemical lemon. I was mostly aware but also not—that state between waking and dreaming—and the pain vacillated between searing and throbbing.

Finally, my husband and father came in to see me. Wes very gently placed his hand over mine.

"Nas," he said, his voice grounding me through the pain.

The police arrived just then. I can't describe them, because my eyes were closed, and to me they were just disembodied voices combined with a sort of groaning sound from the shifting of their big heavy police belts. Wes stood on one side of my bed, holding my hand, and my dad stood on the other as the two police officers questioned me.

"Can you tell us what happened?" said a deep voice.

"I was run over three times, with the tires going over me five times."

"Three times is consistent with what we heard from other witnesses," said a slightly less deep voice. "What do you mean, 'with the tires going over' you 'five times'?"

"The car hit me," I explained to the disembodied voices, "then stopped, then ran me over going forward: front tires one, back tires two. Then the car reversed: back tires three, front tires four. Then the car drove forward again: front tires five. Five times. That's when it stopped, and I was stuck underneath."

Even in such pain, I could describe the whole sequence. There was a pause. "I see," said Officer Deep Voice. "Five times."

As soon as the police left, I immediately asked my dad and Wes to bring the kids in. I ached to see them.

"I don't think that's a good idea, hon," said the nurse who had just walked in.

Not a good idea? They'd been the main thread of my scattered near-death thoughts, and I wanted to reassure them that I was here, and to be reassured that they were there. I was alive, wasn't I? That was all that mattered.

I had no idea what I looked like. I just knew that I wanted to see my kids. How could seeing their mother be a bad idea?

"Please," I said. "I just need to see them."

"Why don't we wait just a little while longer—let you rest?" Westcott said.

"Please?" Pregnant pause. "Please?" I repeated.

Wes left the room, returning a few minutes later with my wide-eyed children. Their footsteps were tentative as they approached. I was smiling—at least in my mind I was. What they saw—well, you can probably imagine. I cracked open the eye that was openable. Asha was calm and composed, standing there with a blank expression. Kaly was behind her, a look of shock on his face. Jasper burst into tears.

"Oh, babe, it's OK," I said. "Hey, look at your new blue cast!" It was a feeble distraction, but Jasper played along, holding up his arm for me to examine. He tried to calm himself down; I could feel him clenching his teeth, trying to hold back the sobs. But it was too much. He couldn't hide the terror and fear no matter how hard he tried.

Wes caught on to my attempt to redirect the focus. "Yeah, he did great in the doctor's office this morning. Not only did he pick the coolest color, but it's waterproof too!"

Kaly continued to cower behind Asha. This was unusual. As my youngest, he was still the cuddliest, the first one to rush in for hugs.

"Kaly?" I said. "Come over here; come hold my hand." He stayed where he was, frozen. Even through my blurry vision, I could see his eyes so wide, so terrified. Asha stepped back and gave him a little nudge. "Go on, Kaly; go sit next to Mom," she said. I tried to say it was OK, that he didn't have to, but he was already on his way toward me. He stood close to me, yet he was almost stiff, motionless. He'd started to cry, too, and couldn't meet my eyes or look at me. My sweet baby boy was scared of me.

After a few more minutes of awkward conversation, Asha came over to the bed and sat down behind me.

"Your hair, Mom," she whispered. "It's all . . . sticky. And there's, like, stuff in it. Rocks and sticks and things. I'm going to put it up."

I could feel her hands, so tentative, smoothing my hair away from my face. My scalp ached, even with this gentlest of touches, but I was grateful. A few minutes later, the kids and my dad left. This was a welcome respite. I was still so tired, and trying to put on a happy face for my family had drained me.

Wes and I sat silently for about ten minutes, and then I remembered real life again. Work. Wes took my phone and started notifying people at my office that I would be out for a few days. I also wanted him to text my new client, the one I had spent the day with, and reassure them.

"Tell them I'll be there if they need anything while they finalize the terms of the deal," I told him. "I don't want there to be any hiccups on this last mile. I'll be back in a day or two. Thursday at the latest."

Wes didn't say anything.

Based on the way I looked—which I still was not aware of—he knew that returning to work Thursday was not realistic.

"Actually, let me do it," I said. He handed me the phone, and I held it up to my face to unlock it. Nothing. Can you believe it? My phone did not recognize me. I had to squint to enter in my code, and my home screen was blurred, as though covered in a thick film of butter. My stomach reeled as I tried to pull up my messages. With a sigh, I handed the phone back to Wes. He put it facedown on the little table next to my bed, then checked our local news to see if the accident had been reported on.

There was a post about the incident on our community Facebook page. He read me the message from our mayor and the responses from others in the community.

We hadn't called anybody besides my brother, my parents, and our close friends Robin and Ethan, so no one knew that I was the one who'd been hit.

Their first concern, understandably, was whether the victim was a child since the accident had happened across from the middle school. The mayor assured everyone it was not a child. Little information was known, so her message was brief and factually accurate: an adult female was struck across from the middle school. That was it; that was all it said. Yet, from that single sentence came a deluge of assumptions. People speculated that the adult female— me—was distracted.

"She was probably on her phone," wrote more than one person.

We couldn't believe it. We read the posts but didn't respond to anything; we just felt angry and disappointed that people—even some we knew—could make such comments.

I stayed behind the same ER curtain throughout the evening. The nurses kept checking on me, and specialists trickled in and out to deliver test results, incredulity in their voices. Eye doctors, plastic surgeons, neurologists, a seemingly endless parade with long gaps in between. They'd assumed the worst. But I had no internal bleeding, no skull fracture, not even one single broken bone. While they were working on my eye, however, the doctor realized there were cuts in my eye, and I would need to have a stent put in my tear duct. The surgeon wouldn't be in for hours, so I was going to have to wait until the next day.

"It's a miracle," people kept saying. "Someone must've been watching over you."

One nurse said, "You must have been saved for a reason," then added, "You'll need to pay it forward."

Pay it forward? The idea of doing anything, let alone paying it forward, overwhelmed me. And I had to find a reason that I'd been saved too?

At around ten o'clock that night, six hours after the accident, I asked Wes to help me to the bathroom. It was the first time I was attempting to get up, and I quickly realized that I could barely stand. Still, nature was calling, so he got me to the bathroom door, and I took it from there.

Inside, in the mirror over the sink, I got my first glimpse of what I looked like. I didn't recognize myself. Cuts and gashes crisscrossed my face, and a plum-purple bruise marred my chin. I had two black eyes, one of which was swollen shut. I couldn't tell if it was rivulets of dried blood running away from that eye like tears, or if those were more cuts. My lips were cracked and grotesquely swollen, like I'd had a seriously botched filler procedure. In fact, every part of my face was swollen and lumpy. The cheek that I had been so worried about was intact, as the EMT had promised, but I couldn't tell the extent of the damage since it was covered by a big beige bandage. I could see the dark blood underneath, and another patch of lacerations below. My neck had another bloody bruise. My hair, which had been pin straight that morning, was sticky, clumped together into little rat's nests despite Asha's efforts. I was a female Indian Frankenstein. No wonder my kids were scared.

I collected myself enough to do my business and get back to the bathroom door, where Wes waited to escort me back to bed. Soon after, the plastic surgeon resident came in. He and Wes gently cleaned my face, dabbing it with warm wet towels while I tried not to gasp in pain. Then he stitched up my upper cheek and eye area as well as my ear where the cartilage was falling out. (I hadn't even noticed the ear in the mirror earlier.)

Finally, around one o'clock in the morning, I asked my husband to leave. "Please," I said. "Go home and take care of the kids."

I was worried about their emotional state and Wes's too. He was clearly exhausted, and though he didn't act like it, I could tell he was hanging on by a thread.

Once Wes left, I just lay in the dark and cried. I couldn't sleep, even with a hefty dose of painkillers and sedatives. My body felt like I was under a weighted blanket full of prickly thorns. I was stiff and immobile, bruised and tender or worse, just raw where the tires had torn off my skin. The slightest move could cause a searing jab.

I knew my bones were intact and there was no internal bleeding, and I was lucky about that. Still, there was no position that offered me comfort; some just offered less pain. I couldn't open my eyes, couldn't bear any light, couldn't even focus my thoughts. I was physically and mentally overwhelmed and exhausted down to my very marrow.

What would the next day bring? My mind went back and forth between reality and fantasy, with longer stop-overs on the fantasy side. I'd seen the Frankenstein face looking back in the mirror, yet I continued to try to think my way back to normality. I was lying down, so I could sort of forget how difficult it'd been to walk to the bathroom, and I imagined that tomorrow I might just roll out of bed. Sure, I'd limp a little, but I'd told my boss I'd be back to work on Thursday, and I was determined to follow through (even though I was the only one fooling myself about fulfilling that promise). I'll just go home and be better, I reasoned.

Life will be back to normal in a few days. My kids will be so relieved. Then I'd carelessly move my arm or turn my head; a sharp pain would snap me back to reality, and I'd start crying again. I was so confused. I had woken up that day as a strong adult woman, and now I felt like a helpless child, alone and scared behind the curtain of an ER.

That night brought little sleep. I heard police officers walking through the ER at all hours, listening to the sound of their leather belts shifting and boots squeaking on linoleum and garbled talk on their radios. In a way, their presence was comforting. Yet sometime in those long dark hours, as I was lying there flat on the gurney, completely immobilized, I overheard two men arguing with each other.

"I'm gonna pop you as soon as we get out of here," threatened the first.

"Nah, man, I'm gonna pop you," responded the second.

This went on for a while. Oh god, I thought. Please don't let this escalate.

Then I heard a woman's voice. "I'm going to pop you both if you don't shut up," she said. I smiled before a shot of pain went through my face. That was some good comic relief in the midst of this nightmare, and it managed to pull me out of my self-pity. They did indeed shut up after her warning, and I got a few hours of sleep.

The next morning, I was still behind that same curtain. I was never officially admitted—since nothing was broken—and Wes found me where he left me. After the eye surgery, I would be released from the ER.

My brother, fresh off a red-eye from San Francisco, joined us later that morning, and my friend Robin also came by to wait with me for eye surgery. There was nothing to do but wait, take painkillers, try to sleep, and try not to cry.

At some point, Robin, a lawyer, suggested a photo shoot. "We should probably get pictures of your injuries, just in case insurance needs it." I was "cleaned up" by then and thought I didn't look too bad, so wasn't sure the pictures would represent the severity of how disfigured I was. Turns out a wet wipe can't transform Frankenstein! The injuries, of course, were very visible.

The eye surgeon was finally ready for me in the middle of the afternoon. Putting the stent in was a quick procedure, barely an hour, and once the anesthesia wore off, I was free to go. Wes, Asha, and Zahid were there to pick me up and take me home. They brought a pair of sweatpants and a big sweatshirt, and Asha gently helped me dress so I could leave the hospital and return home to the boys, looking a little more presentable—or maybe a little less horrific.

My trip to the ER was over. Technically, nothing was broken. I had no internal bleeding, no skull fracture, not a single broken bone. I was lucky.

And I was broken.

CHAPTER

DENIAL. I'M FINE!

> Don't let what you cannot do interfere with
> what you can do.
>
> —John Wooden

When I left the hospital on May 22, 2018, only twenty-four hours after being run over, I went home to my husband, three children, new au pair, two dogs, and one cat, but I may as well have washed up on a deserted island. Everything had changed. I didn't recognize my world. I felt lonely, lost, and isolated—and the enormous ocean of love that surrounded me just made it worse. I didn't want pity; I wanted the power of my mind back.

Up until this point, whenever I ran into a problem, I'd simply figure out the solution. I'd been inspired by Ayn Rand's *The Fountainhead* in my early twenties, and that mentality of self-sufficiency had guided me ever since. I wholeheartedly believed in the strength of the idea that a man's "brain is his only weapon." I'd grown confident in my reasoning mind, in my DIY skills, my ability to weigh the pros against the cons, find a new exit or a new opportunity, then organize and implement a strategy. Maybe it wouldn't be easy, and maybe there'd be some stress involved, but even when a quick fix eluded me, I generally felt like a light bulb would go on eventually. I was not a victim, had never felt like a victim even when life's unfairness presented itself. Next steps were kind of my thing, putting one foot in front of the other, even in the midst of big life ruptures or what seemed to be, at the time, dead ends.

I'd gotten my first lesson in finding a way around big roadblocks my sophomore year of college, when a quarter-life crisis had stomped on me like a big angry boot. My first year of college had been mostly great—I was still insecure, but I also felt so much less like the odd person out.

For one, there were students of all stripes at the University of Maryland, student organizations for Black people and Jewish people and Chinese people, clubs for people who liked fashion or computer science or accounting. Politics tended toward progressive, and every day it seemed like there was a rally or protest to build AIDS awareness, end apartheid, win the right for women to choose. The diversity was refreshing.

For another, I spent much of my college life seeking altered states. (This is difficult for me to admit as my eldest child sets out on her own college adventure, but I don't want to become that thing we all dreaded we'd become after thirty: a hypocrite. Please, oh please, no matter what, stay safe out there! Make better choices!) In some ways, drugs helped me step away from my sense of self, my self-consciousness, and my ego. But more often, it was an analgesic with very short-lived benefits and, sometimes, uncomfortable consequences, the least of which was feeling like garbage the next day. Though it temporarily numbed the symptoms, it didn't actually fix the underlying issue. That would have to wait.

My other coping strategy, which I still use to this day, was . . . shopping. On weekends, I'd scour the Salvation Army for jeans, which I'd take to a tailor to get tapered. With that I'd pair sweaters turned backward to get a low back instead of a scoop neck, or a black bodysuit and mustard blazer from Express, then head out to whatever frat party my friends wanted to go to or to freshman events hosted on campus. Guys had started to notice me, and not in a "you'd be cute if you were white" kind of way.

Sophomore year, however, I pledged Kappa Kappa Gamma. Now, don't get me wrong—there are many good reasons to join a sorority. Built-in network! Decent housing! Great people! Lots of parties! On the other hand, with joining went the expectation that the sorority would be your life and the majority of your identity, and though it did provide an easier route to meeting people and making friends, the people you met and the friends you made were generally part of the Greek system. On top of that, just about everyone at KKG looked pretty similar, and all that color I'd been reveling in the previous year drained from the picture, leaving me, once again, as the conspicuous brown person in a sea of blond.

This prompted the daunting existential question of who I was and what I wanted to be. Everyone else seemed to have it all figured out, or they weren't too concerned with the impending future. There was always another frat party to go to, after all. Though I felt a lot more comfortable in my own skin than I had in high school, I didn't exactly feel confident. I thought I was alone, and was unaware that few twenty-year-olds truly feel confident.

I didn't want to just kill time or, heaven forbid, wait for Prince Charming to swoop me up and bestow upon me an MRS degree. That was not why I was at college. Problem was, I didn't know why I was there. I considered changing schools, changing majors, or simply dropping out and joining the Peace Corps.

One weekend, I took a break from school and went home so I could be miserable in the comfort of my own room. I threw on my favorite pair of pajamas—ratty sweats and an oversized T-shirt with a chocolate ice cream stain, which I would never have dared to wear anywhere else— and spent the majority of Saturday crying in bed. My mom left tea and toast on my nightstand, and every now and then, my dad would peek in, say hello, then escape down the hall. My parents were lovely people who generally tried to avoid all deep, controversial, or complex conversations with me, so when they couldn't take it anymore, they sent in my brother to make it stop.

Zahid came in and sat on the edge of my twin bed, ignoring the mound of soggy tissues at his feet. I don't remember most of what we talked about that afternoon, just that he mostly asked me questions about my life, and I mostly complained about my lack of purpose. He listened with patience, his extra eight years of experience and wisdom painfully obvious. Then he said two things that completely turned me around. First, he said, "Nas, when are you going to finally accept that we are misfits? Once you understand that we are not like other people, you will be a lot happier." Then he said, "Just go to college and learn how to think. Learn how to solve problems and think. That's the only thing you need to do."

My brother was the one who suggested that I check out The Fountainhead, which turned out to be just the book I needed, a book about self-sufficiency, strength, and uncompromising belief in oneself. Zahid's advice lifted the weight of what to do with my life. All I had to do in that moment was go to school and learn how to think. How to think and solve problems. There was my plan, and it worked.

Now, however, my plan didn't work. I couldn't think or solve problems. I had no idea what to do. Everything hurt. I had no plan. I had no next steps. Or I had a million next steps, with no yellow arrow marking the starting point. More than that, I couldn't see. I could stay awake for only short periods of time. I couldn't walk. I couldn't even handle simple questions, like what to have for dinner. I was overwhelmed. I was in pain. I had a stent for the torn tear duct and skin at the inner corner of my eye. I had stitches to sew up the cut above my right eyebrow and the torn cartilage and lobe of my right ear. My face was covered in abrasions, and I had open wounds on my chest and butt and thighs. Open wounds, as in no skin, the raw pink flesh fully exposed. My right breast had been crushed, the pec torn, the skin on and around my nipple torn away. I had several bulging discs. My right hip was swollen and my MCL was torn and my right knee couldn't support my weight. My right hand had that uncomfortable pins-and-needles sensation. My neck, from my trapezius to the top of my ear, had purple streaks of bruising. I felt like I'd been burned, my skin was so raw. I couldn't bear to look at my body—the wounds were so vivid, so grotesque, like the most elaborate zombie-movie special effects. Everything hurt.

Then there was the concussion. I couldn't tolerate light or noise. I had an underlying sense of disorientation. Everything was familiar but, at the same time, alien. My reasoning mind felt opaque, able to work about as fast as butterscotch pudding. And then there was the fear—the mushy mind of concussion is really scary for someone who's used to a high degree of clarity. (What even are we, if not our minds?) I felt completely disconnected from myself.

But I was fine!

I didn't know which doctors to call, what kind of care or follow-up I needed. I had the luxury of having doctors in my family to consult, yet none of them really knew what to do. Where to even begin the process wasn't clear.

First things first: blood was still in my hair. Normally, I washed my hair twice a week and went to the hairdresser every month for a touch-up and a couple of times a year for a Brazilian blowout so that it was straight and shiny with minimal effort. Now, however, my hair was so nasty— that stickiness mixed with grit from the road, the smell of iron and dirt and something worse, something I couldn't bear to identify. This, at least, I could do something about. Except that I could barely move, and my own hair on my own head might as well have been in the next room; it was that far out of reach.

"I'll help you, Mom," my daughter said, a phrase that would become a refrain over the coming days and weeks and months.

This is where my memory blanks out. I've consulted Asha, and hers does too. This forgetting, I would later learn, is a common effect of trauma (not to mention traumatic brain injury, often referred to as TBI). Why we both can't remember the simple act of washing my hair, when there are far more painful memories I'd rather forget, is a mystery.

I can imagine it: Asha pulling a chair over to the kitchen sink, gingerly placing a towel on the back of my neck, helping me lean back against the rim. Holding her hand under the faucet until the water was the right temperature, then grabbing the sprayer. Relief flooding through me as that first soft stream of warm water poured over the crown of my head. Asha massaging shampoo into my hair, the scent of coconut filling the kitchen, Asha being careful not to tug or in any way upset the position of my head. Maybe she asked, "Should I wash your scalp? Or will it sting?"

"Just water for now," I probably told her, through aching lips.

It would take three days and multiple kitchen-sink showers to get all the blood out, and my beautiful, bright daughter, only thirteen years old, helped me each time.

Wes took two weeks off from work. I tried to convince him that I didn't need him to. The au pair was taking care of the kids, and I was planning to go back to work in a couple of days anyway, so what was the point of his staying home?

I was fine!

My family was so sweet, determined to take care of me despite my resistance. Wes and Asha checked on me constantly, asking how they could help. My boys were just as loving and attentive, and I could sense they were aching to find "normal" moments with me. We loved cozying up in front of the TV, and so that was what we did. Or tried to do. I did my best to pretend like it was OK, sitting there on the couch, so bruised and fragile that I couldn't bear to let them get too close, squinting at the light through swollen zombie eyes, trying not to scream or put my hands over my (badly injured) ears to block the sound. Everything hurt.

But I was fine!

It wasn't just my children who were so sweet and loving. Our friends and community were incredibly warm and concerned. Everybody wanted to help me and our family. I was touched that people cared, and at the same time, I was deeply embarrassed that people thought I needed help. I mean, nothing was broken, at least no bones or major organs. I was not immobilized in a hospital bed. I'd been released after less than twenty-four hours. The nurses had made it clear that I was fortunate to be alive, that I'd better get on with paying it forward. My brother had flown across the country to be here. My parents were just minutes away. We had a live-in au pair to drive the kids to school and sports and to make them dinner. My husband, a workaholic just like me, was taking time off to take care of me, for goodness' sake. I was already so lucky. I had so much support. I didn't need help. I didn't deserve help. Because I was fine! How could I be so selfish as to accept help?

My friend Robin put together a meal train, and every day someone dropped off a casserole or muffins or a collection of healthy grains and green salads in containers. People sent gift baskets full of roasted almonds, dried fruits, a variety of cheeses and crackers, plus little tea cookies and truffles. Beautiful bouquets of sunflowers and gerbera daisies brightened every room.

To be honest, I hated it. I was the helper, not the helpee. I was the one who brought bagels or offered to carpool the kids or make a drugstore run for a friend who was sick. I was the one who sent flowers, delivered food, fundraised for important causes.

I asked my family to keep a running list of who brought what, so I'd be able to write thank-you cards, as though these were gravy boats or monogrammed towels off a wedding registry and not basic sustenance for my family. I could not take in this kindness in its purest form, and instead, I felt it as a burden, an emotional debt that I really did not have the energy to repay.

Pay it forward? Please. I couldn't even put on my own socks.

On top of that, I felt obliged to act as hostess when friends stopped by. I'd limp to the door with my cane, smile through cracked lips, say thank you through gritted teeth, attempt conversation. But the question "How are you?" was enough to short-circuit me. The truth was . . . well, I didn't want to be a downer. I didn't want to rehash the accident, or go through my litany of injuries, or talk about the driver and what the hell she was thinking.

How was I? I was fine!

I couldn't move, couldn't function, and could barely open my eyes to look at my phone or read an email, yet I would just tell my kids and husband to relay the message: Thank you, I don't need anything.

A week after the accident, my brother returned to his home on the West Coast to find that Lucy, his great big Bernese mountain dog, was very ill. Lucy was his sunshine, with her loping stride and big brown eyes and that deep Bernese bark that, per the breed, has no bite to back it up. He was devastated. All I wanted to do was help him, and I was at a loss for what to do.

"What can I do?" I kept asking him. "What can I do to help?"

"Nothing," he said, sadness in his voice. "I don't need anything."

That was an unacceptable answer. Of course he needed something. He was in pain, and I loved him, and I wanted to help. Helping him would give me a sense of purpose, a sliver of control in a nonsensical situation. But he insisted there was nothing I could do.

Did I make the connection between my desire to help a loved one who was in pain and the desire of my community to help me? No, I did not.

Wes spent much of his time those first days dealing with logistics. The driver, it turned out, had forced insurance, meaning most companies wouldn't insure her because of her terrible driving record, and she was essentially covered for only the bare minimum. That meant that our auto insurance company would have to foot the bill.

"What do you mean?" I overheard Wes say into his phone. "But we weren't even driving!"

As you can imagine, the insurance company wasn't exactly pleased. That would turn out to be another ongoing battle.

Our primary care physician started coordinating my team of heroes: an orthopedist, physical therapists, neurologists, trauma therapists, and more. This felt good, and right. I had the start of a plan. I began physical therapy one week after the accident. As I could barely get from one room to the next, the physical therapist, Dave, came to the house three times a week. I can hardly remember what we did in those first sessions. I had no range of motion, and my bruises and lacerations were so raw, I couldn't lie on my back or my stomach or my side. It hurt to keep my eyes open for extended periods of time. I was dizzy and nauseated. Even so, I begged Dave to let me get on the Peloton. I'd just been lying around, letting my bike gather dust, and I was terrified of gaining weight. (I know, I know! Let me remind you, again, that I am a product of my generation.)

"I biked every morning before the accident," I'd say, trying to convince him. "The morning of the accident, I did eleven miles in forty-five minutes!"

"No," he'd always say, "you're not ready."

If I could just get back on the Peloton, things would feel like normal. I asked again. And again. He said no. And no.

"Naseem." He finally looked at me and raised his eyebrows. "You can barely walk. You can barely move. And now you want to get on your bike? C'mon. Let's not get ahead of ourselves."

I knew he was completely right, but still, with the same big ego I'd had when the car first hit me, I thought, This is ridiculous.

At this same time, I started seeing my other hero, a trauma therapist. Linda wore rimless glasses, chin-length, curly auburn hair, and had a steadying presence. Her office was in a converted church, with a long white hallway featuring local artists on a regularly changing basis. That first day, black-and-white photos adorned the walls. Inside, a small couch faced the door. There was a bookcase to the right, a chair to the left, and a big notepad on the wall on which she'd draw diagrams of the brain or list the different stages of trauma.

Wes and I had our first session with her on May 29,

eight days after the accident. Just getting to her office took everything out of me, and Wes held tightly to my arm as I hobbled down the hall from the elevator with the support of my cane. I kept the eye that could open trained on the ground, not wanting to look at the faces of those few who passed by.

Once we were seated, I recounted the accident for Linda. For some people, retelling their story can have the effect of retraumatizing them, but for me, it was the opposite: retelling my story reminded me why I was in the state I was in. I was in shock and disbelief and confusion, and going through the details served to anchor me to reality. Yet, when I finished, I had to ask the question that had been plaguing me. I looked over at Wes beside me.

"Did this really happen?"

"Yes, Nas, it happened," answered Wes. "I was there. I saw the whole thing. I saw the car drive over you. I was screaming, 'Stop!'" His breath hitched. "I was screaming and screaming, and she just kept driving. I don't know why she kept driving. But it did, it really did happen."

"Then how am I still alive?"

"I don't know," Wes said. "But you are."

I continued seeing Linda weekly, often by phone, when I felt too tired or depressed or fearful to make it all the way to her office. As this was help I paid for, I did not feel the same weight of emotional debt as friends and family offering to help.

Like in my sessions with Dave, my physical therapist, I was determined to be productive, to find the yellow arrow that would start me on the path toward normalcy. "I need to go back to work," I'd tell Linda. "I need my kids to see that everything is OK."

"I get it," she replied one day. "And you will go back to work. But can you give yourself time to recover first? Your injuries are still really raw. You are clearly still in a lot of pain, both physically and emotionally. Your mobility is limited. You have a concussion—"

"I know that," I interrupted, waving it all away.

"Do you? I know you do intellectually, but I see a denial of what's actually happening."

I shifted in my seat. Even sitting for any length of time was uncomfortable. "What do you mean?" I asked.

"It's really common for people, after traumatic events, to want to forget what happened and just return to the way things were before."

"Well, wouldn't you want that?" I challenged.

"Yes, I absolutely would. Anyone would." She sighed and recrossed her legs. "The thing is, though, you can't go back. No one can. What happened, happened. Your body will heal, but it's not going to be the same body it was before. Your emotions will even out, but you will not forget, and you may continue to have trouble self-regulating, or you might find yourself getting upset by things that you wouldn't have thought twice about before the accident. This is post-traumatic stress. We just don't know what you, what your life, is going to look like."

"So I'm screwed." I started to cry. Before this, I would never have cried in front of a virtual stranger, even a professional who surely saw tears every single day. My ability to control my reactions was limited, which only served to prove her point, which only made me more upset.

There was kindness in Linda's eyes as she said, "No, you're not screwed. But I think an important thing to work on together here, along with practicing recovery tools, is acceptance. You may never look, move, or be the same."

I knew this was true, at least intellectually, as she'd said. But I hated it. I did not want to accept it. I just wanted my eye, my chest, my knee, my face, to heal. I wanted my mind back, the mind that I'd truly believed could figure out a solution to anything.

"Have you heard of kintsugi?" Linda asked early on. I shook my head. "It means 'golden seams' or 'golden mending.' It's a Japanese practice of mending broken ceramics with gold dust, to highlight the cracks instead of hiding them. They're really quite beautiful."

I paused, waiting to hear the connection.

"Think of yourself as a vase that has been broken. That doesn't mean you are permanently broken, just that you are currently in a state of brokenness. You will mend in some form or another, but you won't be able to go back to that exact state of wholeness. You do have a choice here: you can try to hide your cracks, or you can celebrate them for how they make you beautiful."

I went home that day with something that felt almost like a plan. First, I needed to stop pretending. I was not OK. I could not ride eleven miles on the Peloton, drop my kids off at school, work a ten-hour day, come home, and do it all over again. I could no longer do the things that used to come so easily. I needed help.

Not only did I need help, but others also needed to help. I realized that the accident hadn't just happened to me—it happened to my family, my friends, and my community. When I shut them out, when I refused their help, then I was refusing to allow them to participate in the healing process. I was forcing them to be helpless, which, as I very well knew, was a terrible position to be in. Why would I wish that on them, when I was so desperate to escape my own helplessness? People needed to help me, and I would have to learn how to let them.

Maybe this was one version of paying it forward. By allowing people to drive me to doctor's appointments, to simply sit and keep me company, to drop off dinners for my family or go on a Starbucks or ice-cream run was, in fact, giving people a sense of control in a nonsensical situation. Not only that, by allowing people to help instead of fighting it, I would have more energy to recover as well as show appreciation, not from a sense of duty or guilt but with genuine, heartfelt gratitude. Dear friends as well as people I'd only known in passing had surprised me by showing up for me with no expectation beyond my accepting their help. So, guess what? I finally did.

CHAPTER **6**

THE TIPPING POINT

> Have patience with all things, but chiefly
> have patience with yourself.
> —Saint Francis de Sales

A month after the accident, on June 22, I was mobile enough to walk, with the assistance of my cane and my husband, up the steps of the South Orange–Maplewood Municipal Court. It was the start of summer, and the weather was like the day of my accident, only warmer. Now, however, even though I was wearing my biggest pair of Jackie Ohh sunglasses, the afternoon sunshine hurt my eyes, and the blue sky felt oppressive in its brightness. Bandages covered the abrasions on my cheek and the cut above my eyebrow. I couldn't use my right arm, couldn't hold a cup of coffee or zip up a jacket without pain, and I was still taking oxycodone and acetaminophen, still using cream and pads with benzocaine to get some relief. My biggest win was that

I could finally shower by myself, using a stepladder borrowed from the pantry as a bench, though I couldn't shave my legs yet as they were still too raw, not that I could even reach them anyway. Still, one small victory at a time. I left the house on occasion, mainly for doctor's appointments. (That first Thursday had come and gone, and, surprise, surprise, I had not returned to work.) I was definitely not strutting in my five-inch power heels. A few days earlier, physical therapist Dave finally said yes, we could try the Peloton. Hallelujah! I was going bananas without my exercise routine. I wouldn't say that I hopped on; more like I cautiously maneuvered my way on, as though it were a bucking bronco. Once I got my legs around each side of the seat, I took a deep breath.

Phew, I thought, I made it.

Except I couldn't move.

"That's OK," Dave said, his voice gentle. "This is a good start." I tried not to roll my eyes or cry. "Just put your feet on the pedals and see what happens," he continued. "Do not overdo it."

Every day after that, I got on the bike for ten minutes and tried to push the pedals down. At first, I moved them about an inch, rocking them back and forth for a few minutes before exhaustion overtook me. After a week, I finally made a full rotation.

Now I was walking slowly, with a limp and a cane, every step toward the courthouse a painful reminder of those tires driving over my knee, over my hip. The courthouse was beautiful, with redbrick walls and white trim and lots of big windows and an archway over the entrance. We weren't actually required to be there, but Westcott, Asha, and I had wanted to go, each for our own reasons. Asha, I'm pretty sure, was just there to support me.

I'm not totally sure what I was hoping for. I felt no anger, and I was more than ready to give the driver the benefit of the doubt. Honestly, I felt kind of sorry for her—clearly, she didn't have very good judgment. And we all make mistakes. She hadn't gotten in touch—likely per her lawyer's instruction—and maybe today was a chance for some kind of connection, or some clarity, or closure. I still felt confused about the whole thing.

Wes, meanwhile, was pissed. This was very, very unlike him. The only time I'd ever seen him angry in our twenty years together was when I shaved his hair before a job interview and accidentally gave him a bald spot. Oops!

That was the only time I'd ever heard him yell.

Now, he was playing it semicool, but I could see the anger simmering beneath the surface. He was the one who'd said at the accident, "Don't you even care what happened to her?" and gotten no response. He'd seen the driver sitting on the curb, crying into her phone, more concerned with herself than with the person under her car. She'd never even walked over to check on me. So he was probably less surprised by what came next.

Inside the courthouse was chaos. We didn't know where to go, so we just stood in the same long line as everyone else, assuming it would take us to someone who'd point us in the right direction. We waited anxiously, Westcott using his height to peer over the crowd, me leaning against my husband and trying to breathe through the discomfort. My body hurt, and the noise around us, the movement and chatter and footsteps on stone created a cacophony that made my head throb. I felt nausea rising in my throat and exhaled with intention as Linda had taught me. After a few minutes, we heard someone calling the driver's name, and we saw her, not ten feet away. That was the first time I saw her. She was in her early sixties, of average height and weight, and the definition of "unassuming." Nothing about her expression or posture connected with the screaming I'd heard when she'd stepped out of the car, that screaming that was wholly self-focused, wholly unconcerned with the person she'd hurt. She looked like anyone.

I took the man next to her to be her lawyer. He had a suit, a briefcase, and a deep side part in his gray hair.

"Don't worry," he said to her as they approached. "We'll get you out of this."

Um, excuse me? I looked at Westcott and Asha. Their eyes were wide with shock. "What the fuck," Wes said under his breath. He was practically shaking, he was so angry.

In the courtroom, we took a seat in the wooden pews and waited. And waited. Most of the people were there for standard traffic violations. After a million years, the bailiff called our driver. The judge furrowed his brow as he looked over the paperwork.

"How do you plead?" he asked.

"Not guilty," she answered.

Her lawyer stood up. "I would like to request a continuance on behalf of my client," he said.

Then they left.

Asha, Westcott, and I stayed where we were, frozen. The driver and her lawyer did not look in our direction as they walked down the aisle toward the door. The bailiff called the next case, and that was it. It was over.

I swallowed a sob. This was in no way the image I'd had in mind of how this day would go. I was a devout follower of the Golden Rule, a big believer in karma and personal responsibility. You make a mistake, and you own up to it, make amends, move on. You do a bad thing, intentionally or not, and you own up to it, make amends, move on. How could she plead "not guilty"? In what universe is someone who hits a person with her car, stops, drives forward, backs up, and drives forward again not guilty? I felt that sob I'd swallowed rising in my chest, trying to force its way out in the form of a scream. Never before had I felt so . . . helpless. So confused. So angry.

I couldn't keep it together anymore. I'd been standing there, not ten feet away, with my bandages and sunglasses and cane, and the person who had hurt me hadn't even bothered to acknowledge me. Even if she didn't recognize me, she had seen my husband. She had exchanged words with Westcott. She'd run over me. I'd been completely invisible to her on May 21, and I was completely invisible now. I was run over yet again. All these weeks of pain, of being unable to see straight, of losing my most basic sense of who I was—invisible. Rage turned over in my stomach, a horrible, hot sensation that left me panting. Wes put his hand on my arm, and I could feel the tension in his fingers, his effort to hold himself together. "C'mon," he said, helping me to my feet. "Let's go talk to the prosecutor."

We watched the prosecutor, a fortysomething man in a suit that had seen better days, as he gathered up his paperwork, then tailed him at my snail's pace into the hallway. He entered a conference room, conspicuously not noticing us, a bandaged woman in big sunglasses flanked by a man clenching his jaw and a lost-looking teenager. A court officer stood in front of the door. "Excuse me," Wes said. "Can we speak with the prosecutor?"

The officer looked at us blankly. "No, sir," he said.

"Please." Wes gestured to me and Asha. "We just need a minute."

After more urging, the officer finally sighed. "I'll see what I can do."

"I don't have time to talk to you," the prosecutor said as we approached him. This man was clearly ready for a career change.

Wescott insisted. "My wife was the one who was run over by the car."

The prosecutor glanced at me, taking in my cane, my sunglasses, the bandages on my face. "Fine," he said. "What do you want me to do about it?"

"I don't know," Wes said, "but this was not a minor traffic violation. The driver should at least lose her license or something!"

"Listen; that's not how it works," he said, his tone dripping with condescension. I cringed. Why was he speaking to us as though we were the ones at fault, as though we weren't the victims, as though we had been tried and found guilty? "Now if you'll please excuse me."

We walked out of the courthouse in silence. The late-June sunshine was like a razor on my eyes. I felt sick. Wes and Asha practically had to carry me down the courthouse steps to our car. I tried to hold it together, but I couldn't help but let the tears fall once the door was closed and we were in motion, my husband driving slowly through the parking lot, gripping the steering wheel so tight, his knuckles were white.

I lost it when we got home. Everything Wes and the kids did grated on my nerves, and the au pair could do nothing right. Kaly had the gall to ask to go to the public pool on a gorgeous summer day, and boy, did I let him have it. Jasper, unloading the dishwasher, dared to put a dish away in the wrong spot, and I didn't hold back on pointing out his egregious mistake.

There was still a teeny-tiny sliver of self-awareness, a part of me floating above a strange scene in which a scarred, sobbing woman screamed at her children. These children had been forced to grow up so fast in the last few weeks, and they'd done everything they could to take care of me. Asha helped me dress, helped get her brothers ready for school. They all brought me water, kept me company, asked if I needed anything. Whoa, that part of me wanted to say to the rest of me, I think maybe you're taking your feelings out on the wrong people. But the rest of me, the much larger part that was disoriented and in pain, furious at her new self, her new life, was not listening. I was like a toddler having a tantrum—all sense of control, of scale, had left me. Screw the golden seams of kintsugi, everything was broken and awful.

I finally calmed down, exhaustion snuffing out my anger. I sat alone, in my darkened bedroom, when it hit me what I had just done. All that love and gratitude I'd felt while under the car, my unspoken vow to make sure the people I loved knew that I loved them, to never take my life for granted, had been eclipsed, forgotten. My kids were afraid of me.

In 2001, Wes and I eloped in Fiji. (It was a planned elopement, with our parents' blessings.) It was there and then, during one of the happiest weeks of my life, that I mustered up the courage to learn how to swim. Remember that pool my parents had that I didn't learn to swim in? Now I had to let Wes know that his soon-to-be wife had never jumped in the ocean before!

I'd never left the shallow end of my parents' pool, and even though I'd grown up a short car ride from the beach, I'd never dared to venture into deep waters, only wading in enough to cool down on the hottest August afternoons. Now, surrounded by the most dazzlingly clear-blue seas, high on romance and bright green mangos and soursop cocktails, I was ready to take the leap.

Wes and I snorkeled the day before our wedding; I wore a life jacket, so I could see every color in the entire world, paddling at the surface above clownfish and sea turtles and anemones waving in the current. The rest of the week, we took a scuba certification course, during which the instructor conveniently turned his head when I took the swimming test. An open shark dive was the obvious next step. The shark guides tell you, explicitly, not to flail. Erratic movement like, say, that of an injured octopus, gets a shark hyped up and is therefore the last thing you want to do. No problem for Wes. I, on the other hand, did not have enough skill to swim without flapping about like a floundering flounder, so my brand-new husband held me close.

Years later, Wes would carry our kids on his back into the water while I watched nervously from the shore. Swimming, it turns out, is not a skill that develops organically—you actually have to seek out bodies of water and then submerge yourself in them in order to practice.

I did not like being left stranded on the beach, excluded from the fun and unavailable should my husband and children need me, so I bit the bullet and signed up for swim lessons. Because what if my kids were drowning, and I couldn't save them?

Now I felt like I was drowning. And I was pulling my family down with me.

My doctor and my therapist, Linda, had both been suggesting that I start antianxiety and antidepression medication, and I'd been adamant that I did not need it. I was strong and mentally tough—I'd just think my way out of this. My reasoning mind and all that! I didn't need pharmaceuticals!

I was raised on self-sufficiency and independence, on the American dream of blood, sweat, and bootstrapping, then reaping the rewards. My mother was the very model of the hardworking immigrant, always keeping herself together. After coming home from her long days at work, an Indian woman in a white man's world, she would start the second shift, take off the pumps, and put on the chappals— my dad wanted a good Indian wife who cooked, and so that was the wife she would be. (I know, I know! Remember, she was a product of her generation too.) She was the most competent, composed person I knew, the kind of person who got the party started and cleaned up afterward.

My mom never showed weakness, and so neither my father nor I recognized the changes when her health started to decline. At a party in 2008, just a few months before Kaly was born, a close friend of my parents, a neurologist, took my dad aside and said, "I think Sena has Parkinson's."

Did my mom notice a tremor in her hand, a stiff leg that made walking more difficult? I don't know—she never said anything.

She was officially diagnosed soon after that, but we never really talked about it. She never brought it up, never complained. She also never held Kaly standing up. She silently recognized the changes. As the disease progressed, I'd ask her about what was happening, and she'd maybe outline some new challenges, but she'd never say, "I'm miserable," or "I can't believe this is happening," or "Why me?" She certainly never asked for help. Occasionally, with utter frustration, my dad would call me or my brother, Zahid, and report that she'd dropped the remote control and, instead of calling him over, had tried to pick it up and fallen herself. Her effort to not be a burden would backfire.

My dad didn't like to talk about her illness and their new reality either. They were that power couple, the stockbroker and the hematologist-oncologist, the social butterflies who went to four parties a week and traveled the world (probably eating fancy gourmet ice cream), making friends wherever they went.

"How's Mom?" I'd ask him.

"Oh, she's fine," he'd answer. "She's fine."

My mom never showed weakness. All those years of the kind of superhuman strength necessary to be a working mother in a home with more traditional gender roles, her juggling everything, taking care of everything, getting buy-in from my dad—that's a hard habit to break. We saw my parents often, and, yes, we noticed that maybe my mom was leaning on my dad a little more or needing a hand to get up from the couch, but these issues seemed minor. No big deal. But the year of my accident, 2018, she began using a wheelchair. Here was evidence that her world was getting smaller and smaller, that she was trapped in a body that was failing her.

So who was I to complain? After ten years of her nearly silent suffering, the severity of her disease was no longer deniable. My body hurt; my head hurt; my thoughts and emotions were out of control. But I knew, at least theoretically, that I would heal to some degree. Whereas my mom would not.

I was clearly not as strong as how I saw my mother. The guilt of this, of feeling like my struggle was somehow self-indulgent when compared with hers, did not help or inspire me to "just get over it." I was broken and, on top of that, I was ashamed of my brokenness. But I had a family that needed me. My mom needed me, even if she never said so. My dad needed me, even if he himself didn't know it.

That terrible day in court was the tipping point. My family had been dealing with it for several weeks, and now I had no choice but to admit it. I just couldn't process my feelings or make sense of what was happening to me. I couldn't understand how the driver could show no remorse or simply ignore me, and I couldn't understand how to truly deal with my new reality. And my kids were suffering because of it.

I called my doctor. I told her I was ready to start the meds, though I wasn't, not really. I felt weak and disappointed in myself, but that was outweighed by how I'd been treating my children. They were afraid of me, this new person who couldn't control her emotions, who screamed at them for no reason. On top of that, I wasn't setting a good example. I wanted my own kids to feel comfortable receiving help when they truly needed it, not to have this internal struggle that created disconnection and ultimately only made life harder for everyone. My kids' friends and teachers, my friends like Robin and Maria, had been so wonderful, so caring and open and understanding, so generous in their support—would I want my kids to feel guilty about that? Of course not.

This was not the mom I wanted to be. This was not the kind of childhood I wanted to give my kids. And if a prescription could get me to a functional approximation of myself again, that would be good enough.

CHAPTER 7

TOO SOON

Fearlessness is not the absence of fear.
Rather, it's the mastery of fear.
—Arianna Huffington

Between my various doctor's appointments and the four-teen to sixteen hours of sleep I needed, I often felt like my entire life was a testament of my brokenness. I was so over my cane, so over my pain, so over my bandages and ice packs and antibacterial ointments and heating pads and knee brace and vitamin E oil and neck pillows and eye drops and compression bands and scar gels. One minute I'd think, *Kintsugi! Golden seams! There's beauty in brokenness!* and the next I'd think, *Another nap? Another pill? Another waiting room? When am I going to get my real life back?*

Despite the warnings of every sane person in my life, whether it was my doctors, my dad, Zahid, Robin, Jasper, or my boss—or his boss—I was dead set on returning to work eight weeks after the accident. That terrible day in court hadn't altered my stance. In fact, I was more determined to just get on with it. At least then I wouldn't be sitting at home all day, ruminating about the driver's attitude and the inhumanity of the "justice system" and all the other million things that I couldn't change. "I'd recommend you stay home another month or two, until you're stronger," my doctors said. "Give your head injuries a little more time to heal. What's another month or two, in the grand scheme of things?"

What's another month or two? I could tell you: It's too much. Way too much. I wasn't someone who took time off! A couple of years after 9/11, I'd wanted to do more to show that stereotypes about Muslims were wrong, and so I applied to the Columbia Graduate School of Journalism. My acceptance letter arrived when I was five months pregnant with Asha; Wes and I were in the middle of building a crib, and I put aside my screwdriver so I could open the envelope with shaking hands. Both of us were making respectable salaries, and I had finally reached a place where I felt confident and proud of myself. Full-time job plus graduate school plus a baby? Why the heck not?

I went into labor during an eight-hour Saturday class. The teacher had put the fear of God in us about missing this class, and so I sat there, trying to take notes and keep my breathing steady. Only my three girlfriends knew what was happening, and they covertly helped me time my contractions as the clock ticked on. (I really, really didn't want to be a distraction to the class!) The contractions were pretty far apart, so I wasn't panicked. At the end of the day,

Wes picked me up, and as soon as I'd buckled my seat belt, I said, "I'm in labor."

"Great!" he said. Then his phone rang, a friend calling. After they chatted for a minute, he said, "Want to come over for a barbecue?"

"Hey," I interrupted, nudging his arm. "I'm in labor, remember?"

"Oh, right," he whispered to me, returning to his phone call. "Rain check."

Asha was born about twenty-four hours later after a long, painful back labor with an ultimate C-section. She was a beautiful healthy little girl, and I only missed one class at school, though I did take a twelve-week maternity leave from my job. By the time I graduated from Columbia, I was pregnant with Jasper, and left journalism behind. After his birth and the birth of Kaly—both of whom were preemies—I did not take any time off work. Before you assume anything, you should know I didn't feel like I needed to. We had a nanny, who could more than handle two, then three, children, and I was in sales, a role with built-in flexibility. My customers trusted me to work at my own pace, on my own schedule. I juggled it all.

I realize I had more support and more resources than most. I made choices I was comfortable with at the time, and I was blessed with an abundance of energy and willpower. That's where I was coming from when I thought, if I could give birth and then keep going full steam ahead, then I could easily go back to work eight weeks after an accident. No broken bones? No skull fractures? No internal bleeding? I was fine!

More than anything, I wanted to feel normal again,

wanted to be the equal provider for my family I'd always been. I was more than ready to ignore the doctors' advice and my own body's signals in order to make it happen.

One day in the third week of July, I decided that enough was enough. I was sitting in yet another hospital waiting room the Friday before I was scheduled to return to work. I was alone, as I had finally been cleared to drive, and I'd been twiddling my thumbs for about thirty minutes, waiting to do some breast-imaging tests. I could see that my breasts didn't match, but I also questioned my own perception—my eyes didn't match either. Plus I was so focused on all the scars around my breast, perhaps that was distorting my view. Was it superficial, or was there something deeper, something worse going on?

Actually, I wasn't sure I wanted to know.

I stood up. I saw the receptionist look up from her computer out of the corner of my eye and, before she could say anything, I grabbed my purse and walked out. Outside, I took out my phone and proceeded to cancel that appointment and several others that were lined up for the day. Behind the wheel of my blue Mini Cooper Clubman, I took a moment to catch my breath. Where to? I had no idea. Then my stomach rumbled. An idea popped into my head.

I pressed the ignition start button. I still walked with a cane and still had to wear big sunglasses to shield my eyes from the light, but I felt ready to make the twenty-mile drive into New York City, to Dos Caminos, my favorite Mexican restaurant in the Meatpacking District.

I got a table for one outside and ordered some chips and guacamole and a spicy margarita, extra salt. The guacamole came in one of those heavy mortar and pestles, with warm tortilla chips fresh out of the oven. It had been almost two months since I'd had a drink, and the first lick of salt off the rim followed by the first sip out of the straw made me so happy, like maybe I might be "me" again, if not now, then soon. My first crunchy bite of chips and guacamole brought me back to the day before the accident, when I was that busy mom catching some quality time with her middle child, as light and carefree as someone with a full-time job, three children, and an endless list of weekend activities and errands can be. I'd felt so in control, so on top of my bottomless to-do list. In that moment, with that first gulp of tequila warming my belly, the gap between who I was and who I had been seemed surmountable.

Asha and one of her girlfriends happened to be in the city that day, putzing around and getting dessert at some Instagram-worthy restaurant, so I called them to offer a ride home later. I was proud of my accomplishment and my chutzpah, of blowing off the doctor and coming into NYC. I'd even talked to therapist Linda during the drive and told her as much before cutting the session short.

Soon after I ended the call with my daughter, however, I realized that one margarita after two months' sobriety and antidepression/antianxiety medication didn't exactly mix. Tequila, tortilla, and guacamole roiled in my belly.

Uh-oh, I thought. Looks like I'm wasted.

I stood up on shaky legs, grabbed my bag, and, using my cane, raced (slowly and carefully) down the stairs to the restroom, where I threw up all the delicious Mexican food I'd just eaten. At the sink, I washed my hands, wiped off my sunglasses, and rinsed out my mouth, then caught a look at myself in the mirror. The scars on my face were still fresh, pearlescent pink against my skin.

I called Wes. "Hi, hon," I said. "I'm drunk. Can you come rescue me?"

Luckily, he was at work in NYC and could take the train downtown to meet me.

Can you believe how ridiculous I was? I'd ditched a doctor's appointment and driven into the city for a salty marg and some chips and guac, to prove that I was strong and independent, dammit, and here I was, a damsel in distress calling up her knight in shining armor for a ride. "Maybe don't go back to work yet?" he said when I stumbled into the passenger seat of my car.

But my kids needed normalcy; I needed normalcy. As planned, I returned to work the following Monday, which happened to involve flying to Vegas. Did I feel up to it? Not exactly. But I was determined to be positive, to be grateful, to focus on the joy of survival as I boarded the plane, where I'd be attending a conference with my sales team. They, too, were part of a work culture of positive bias. We were encouraged to press forward with the belief that we would eventually achieve whatever we set out to do. That's what the tech industry thrives on—the only way we will invent and sell entirely new technologies is if we believe we can. I was excited to see my new colleagues again, especially after my win on the day of the accident, which we hadn't had a chance to celebrate. I was excited about reentering my role on a professional high point. Plus the theme of the sales conference was "Ready," and I liked the idea that I was going to be *ready* at Ready. In my clearly ill-functioning mind, Vegas was the perfect place to cele-brate my return!

I'd been to Sin City many times and always loved it. I loved staying out all night at clubs, downing a free drink or two, playing blackjack, and feeling sure that Lady Luck would smile down on the next hand. Even if she didn't, I felt lucky when I was there, thriving in all that neon and festive hustle. That was my memory of the place, airbrushed with an overarching sense of happiness. Good times!

That morning at home, I stood in front of the bathroom mirror. My face was healing; the swelling had gone down so that it no longer looked lumpy; the sutures had dissolved; the gashes had mended. My eye with the stent looked the same as the uninjured eye, though both looked more tired than I could remember. Sadder too. But I had a plan. I shook the tube of liquid gold glitter I'd bought especially for this moment.

Kintsugi, I thought, unscrewing the top. If I can't hide the cracks, I might as well make them beautiful. Slowly I traced the lines above my left eyebrow, from my left eye to my left ear, over the rough patch on my right cheek. I turned my head from side to side, assessing my work from different angles. It was beautiful, in its way, a subtle spar-kle that I hoped would create a pleasant distraction—that people would notice the glitter underneath the Jackie Ohh sunglasses, not the scars.

The plane ride itself was the first gauntlet. It was the first time since the accident that I really had no control of my environment. I'll admit to you that I took a Xanax be-fore boarding. I'm not claustrophobic or afraid of flying, and this was a couple of years before the world developed an intense phobia of airborne viruses. I'd never had much trouble with seat size—I'm five feet one, and, unlike for my tall husband, leg room and seat room had never been an issue. I'd also never noticed how loud a plane is—even when it's quiet. That whoosh of the big metal tube hurtling through space, the hum of the engine, and the hiss of the ventilation system combined to make a roar in my head. Fortunately, the light was dim, but no matter what I did, I couldn't get comfortable. My neck and back hurt sitting; my neck and back hurt standing. It was a full flight, too, and I caught people staring as I stood up and sat down, stood up and sat down, giving my body a break from one position and then the other.

It was 108 degrees when we landed. My knee complained as I walked through the tunnel into the airport in my stupid flats. My power platforms and fabulous heels were gathering dust at home, and I was wearing some practical shoes that I absolutely hated. Though I was no longer raw like a burn patient, I couldn't bear to look at my wounds; my outfit covered me from head to toe to protect the scars on my legs, ankles, and breasts. I wore an elbow brace to help with the nerve damage on my right arm, and I soon discovered that walking with a cane while dragging a suitcase is a lot harder than it looks.

Despite two months of not working out, I was still relatively small and skinny, but I was no longer the fit, fabulous woman who got second looks strutting down the street. Well, I did get second looks, but it wasn't from men appreciating my feminine charms. Instead, people stared and, I assumed, tried to figure out what had happened to me. What was with those scars under the sunglasses? Why did someone so young have a cane? Even the most fashionable black cane didn't change the fact that I couldn't walk straight, that I needed help up the stairs to the shuttle bus.

Twenty-five hundred miles from South Orange, and I couldn't call my husband to come rescue me. With the desert sunshine promising a raging headache, the fact that I was ill equipped to return to life slapped me hard in the face.

Thirty minutes later, the bus pulled up at the entrance to the Luxor Hotel and Casino. I leaned heavily on the railing as I stepped down onto a dusty white sidewalk that seemed to have absorbed all the day's heat and then some. Sweat broke out along my hairline, and I adjusted my sunglasses to fully shade my eyes. The driver unloaded my suitcase and pulled out the handle for me. I gave him a few bucks tip, and then I was alone, among a throng of salespeople and gamblers, tourists and casino workers.

A draft of air-conditioning welcomed me inside, where I checked in, smiling at the front desk clerk despite my self-consciousness, and went up to my room. I can do this, I told myself. I put my suitcase in the closet, then looked at the bed with pure longing. Oh, how I wanted to sink into the mattress, to let my throbbing head rest on one of those perfectly plump pillows. If I did, however, I might never get up, and I couldn't waste time resting. I was here to work, dammit. So I rallied, freshening up in the pristine bathroom and heading out to catch the shuttle to the MGM Grand Conference Center for our first meeting. I can do this, I repeated to myself.

I was utterly exhausted by the time I made it down to the shuttle pickup. How was I going to make it through my first meeting, let alone an entire day of meetings? I had no idea.

Again, the driver helped me on and off the shuttle. The blast of hot air between the drop-off area and the conference center entrance hit me hard. Again, the air-conditioning inside was a blessed relief, but otherwise the space was not an improvement. In fact, it was torture. This was Las Vegas, the land of flashing lights, loud music, booming voices over the sound system, big crowds—all the bells and whistles and then some to generate excitement. What was I thinking, coming here?

Before the accident, I would have dived right in. Now, however, my concussed brain simply could not handle it.

My memory of the first conference session is a blur. Afterward, I met some colleagues at the bar. My boss took one look at me and said, "You know, you don't have to come back yet."

Those words would have been annoying the last few weeks, but in this moment, I could only be grateful. My boss knew how dedicated I was, how I'd fought to come back when everyone was telling me to take more time, and it was nice to be let off the hook. "Thank you," I said, relief and disappointment battling for dominance within me—I did not want to be this person, the woman with the cane and antidepressants and scars. But I was.

All I had to do was get back to my hotel room. I decided to walk rather than wait for the shuttle—it was just a few blocks from the MGM Grand to the Luxor, and I was dying to get out of there. By now my nervous system was fully overwhelmed, from the long flight and the logistics of travel and the sights and sounds and oppressive heat of Las Vegas. Of having to be "on." Well, trying to be "on" and fooling no one.

I can do this, I told myself yet again as I set out down the sidewalk, visions of that big cozy bed dancing in my head. I paused at the first crosswalk. Cars zoomed past, just-washed BMWs and Jeeps jostling with dusty Kias and Ford F-150s. Everything was going too fast, like film on fast-forward. The world spun around me, making me dizzy. I closed my eyes and took a deep breath, tried to sense my feet in their stupid flats on the ground. A cacophony of pop and rap and rumba and talk radio booming from open car windows and the whirling sound of tires meeting pavement and voices getting louder as people approached, and softer as they passed by, filled my head. I felt tears of frustration and confusion gathering behind my eyelids. I squeezed my eyes shut even tighter, letting a couple of tears pour over and wiping them away underneath my sunglasses. It's just a street, I told myself. I've crossed a million streets before. I'll be walking with all these people. It'll be fine.

The pedestrian sign turned green. The crowd surged forward. I stayed put, feeling like I might be sick.

The sign turned red. I was alone for only a few seconds before more pedestrians gathered around to wait for the light to turn again. I gripped my cane tightly, determined to cross this time, dammit. Cars and trucks and buses zoomed by. My heart raced. Deep breath, deep breath. The air was boiling hot, full of exhaust fumes. Tight grip, feet on the ground, exhale, exhale.

The sign turned green. I stepped forward. People stepped around me, rushed past me. I focused on my steps, and the bloop-bloop sound of the walking signal.

Bloop, step, bloop, step.

Breathe in, breathe out, I heard Linda say in my head.

My gaze darted to the waiting traffic, looking for a

rogue car breaking out of the line to mow me down. Tears poured down my face, hidden behind my sunglasses. I can do this, I can do this, I can do this.

For the next thirty-six hours, I lay in the darkened room, the air conditioner cranked up high, the white duvet pulled up to my chin, the "Do Not Disturb" sign hung on the doorknob outside. Every so often, I'd dip into a little bag of Starbucks almonds I'd bought in the airport—I really didn't have much of an appetite—and I talked to my family whenever they called.

"Everything's fine," I told them. What else could I say? I didn't want them to worry, and I didn't want to hear the dreaded words "I told you so." Other than those brief, false conversations, my world was quiet, the only sound the air conditioner's hum and, every now and then, the noise of people having fun as they made their way down the hall to their rooms. My mind was quiet, a state I so rarely attained, and my thoughts sort of slid through in slow motion, not quite catching my full attention.

A memory from a couple of weeks back played and re-played like a movie. Though my physical therapist, Dave, had advised against doing too much, I'd decided that a walk on flat ground would do me good. To protect me against the too-bright world, I'd put on my sun hat and Jackie Ohh sunglasses, grabbed my cane, and headed out to a little park with a short trail by my house. The heat hadn't hit yet, and I breathed in the early-morning air, savoring the moment of solitude.

My family and kids and friends like Robin and Maria were all amazing, but it felt wonderful, essential, to be alone, where I didn't have to even attempt to pretend. I

walked slower than I could ever remember walking, because I had to. My mind, too, was operating at a slower
pace, and for once I was slowed down enough to really take
in my surroundings. How long had it been since I'd heard,
really heard, birds singing their morning songs? When was
the last time I looked ahead at the trees in the distance
without clocking steps or calories burned or some other
metric of productivity? Beside the path, a cluster of dandelions had popped up next to a bench. A couple were still in
bloom, that bright, buttery yellow burst. Others had turned
to those white seeded puffballs. I recalled that as a kid, I'd
loved to blow on dandelions and make a wish as the wind
carried the seeds away. How long had it been since I'd done
that? How long had it been since I'd found such pure, easy
joy in anything? I had sat down on the bench and, carefully,
leaned over to pick one of the puffballs. Holding it up to my
face, I had closed my eyes, made a wish, and exhaled.

That memory carried me until Wednesday afternoon, when I rallied enough to put on my gold glitter and
get ready to meet my teammates for cocktails. From the
cool dark cave of my room, I stepped out into the hall, then
slowly made my way to the rooftop bar. Way up high above
the city, with the blare of a million casino lights rolling out
toward a dusk-painted expanse of desert, I ordered something ice-cold and fruity. That first sip: heaven.

The fifth sip and I was done.

A coworker helped me to a seat while another one
brought me a glass of ice water. I drank it down in big gulps,
keeping my eyes closed against the muted light. "I'll walk
you back to your room," another coworker kindly offered.
So much for a fun night out.

It was time to abort the mission, to admit defeat, to

recognize what everyone else, and probably you, already had. A trip to the loudest, booziest, brightest place on earth was a terrible idea. I got my flight moved up to the next day and arrived at the airport early, glad that I was beating the post-conference exodus. Networking was such a crucial part of these conferences, a part I'd previously enjoyed, but now I didn't have the energy to make small talk as I waited for the plane; it was all I could do to grab a coffee, slump back in one of those hard polyurethane seats, put on my big sunglasses, and close my eyes.

CHAPTER 8

QUESTIONS AND
CONNECTIONS

I can be changed by what happens to me.
But I refuse to be reduced by it.
—Maya Angelou

The next day, after coming home from the conference, I worked from home, the kids and the au pair bustling in the rest of the house. This was before the pandemic and WFH became standard practice, so I was grateful that my boss understood my need to do my job from the comfort of my quiet, naturally lit home office. I could've taken another sick day, but it was July, the fiscal time of year when we were busy doing account planning, and I didn't want to miss this chance to collaborate with my colleagues. Though I'd left work on a high note with a big contract to celebrate, I was still the new kid on the team, and I felt the need to prove myself, to prove my dedication. This was wholly self-imposed, mind you—everyone would have completely supported my following my doctors' advice and taking more time to recover.

That following Monday, I returned to the office in New York City. As per usual, I took the Morris and Essex train in and got off at Penn Station. Immediately, I was overwhelmed—by the crowds, by the sound of a million footsteps and a million conversations, by the lights and the bright lettering on the departure boards, by the smells of to-go coffees and fast-food breakfast sandwiches and perfume and sweat. Outside the station was no better. The walk up Eighth Avenue in the morning heat was less than half a mile but required the crossing of eight—I counted—busy streets. I felt claustrophobic and yet comfortable in the middle of the pack as I stepped out into each cross-walk, my chest constricting, my vision tunneling.

Arriving at work in a state of panic did not set the tone I'd been hoping for. More than anything, I wanted to seem normal to my colleagues. I didn't want to regress to feeling different, being the misfit.

Breathe in, breathe out, I told myself, picturing Linda's kind face as I steadied myself.

From that day on, I attended my regular meetings and client calls. Most people were very nice about my absence. Microsoft, like most big global tech companies, has a reputation for working its employees hard. While this is true—and that's why they compensate us well—I was fortunate that my boss and colleagues gave one another plenty of respect and autonomy, the philosophy being that as long as you got the job done, your time was your own, and no one got punished for extenuating circumstances.

Though, they also needed to know the gravity of those

circumstances. One person said to me, "I hope you had a nice time off with your family." I was taken aback. Did she think I was out on vacation? That I was sunbathing and sipping piña coladas at the Jersey Shore? That I was home watching soap operas in the bath?

It wasn't unreasonable that colleagues wanted a particular kind of answer and so asked a particular kind of question such as "Are you back to 100 percent?"

For one, they didn't know me all that well yet. I was still the new kid. And sometimes, people don't really want to know, not because they don't care, but because they feel uncomfortable or helpless or don't want to intrude. I mean, they could plainly see that I was not 100 percent: limp, cane, scars, sunglasses. Yeah, the gold glitter was cute, but still.

I struggled with how to respond. I didn't want to say either yes or no. I wanted people to know how I was, that I might need a little extra leeway, while at the same time it had been my decision to come back to work, a decision I had to admit might have been a poor one. I realize now that my returning to the office after only eight weeks put my colleagues in an awkward position. If I was going to show up and take responsibility for my work, then they were relying on me to do my job and do it well.

And I just wasn't there yet. It took all my stamina to simply be awake for a full eight to ten hours. Staying alert, listening attentively and solving problems, not to mention being clever and charming with clients as is required in sales—that was just beyond me. I felt like I was trying to run up a mountain in those gorgeous power heels I could no longer wear.

I talked about the accident only when asked—which

was pretty much all the time. But I was glad when people asked. That was actually much better than people pretending they didn't notice anything different about me, or seeming embarrassed for me or, heaven forbid, pitying me. I much preferred colleagues and clients to acknowledge that I was dealing with some unusual challenges—that acknowledgment made it so I didn't have to pretend. Every time I told the short version, jaws dropped. Then came the waterfall of questions. Let's pretend you're my coworker:

"Oh my gawd!" you say. *"How did you survive?"*

I did not have a good answer for that. Honestly, I still couldn't quite wrap my head around the fact of the accident. I often asked myself, or Wes, or Linda, if the accident had actually happened. It was so unreal. Sometimes, I'd offer up a theory: Starbucks saved my life. No, seriously.

I'd been drinking chai or coffee lattes almost every day for the previous sixteen years, and I credited the "chai diet"—which essentially meant replacing breakfast or lunch with a chai latte—for losing my pregnancy weight after all three babies. One, or occasionally two, lattes every day added up to seventy ounces of milk per week. That's a lot of calcium! I bet that made my bones strong enough to maybe bear up against the SUV's weight.

On top of that, I'd given up my go-to cheeseburgers and steaks a few years before, after a vegetarian work friend convinced me to go without meat on a business trip to Singapore and India. I'd gotten home feeling good and without the extra weight I usually gained on those trips.

Linda, my therapist, also had a theory. She believed

the success high from my great client meeting that day gave me whatever strength I needed to live. Who really knows, though; it still baffles me. Maybe it was all of these: a healthy diet, strong bones, and hope for my future.

"Oh my gawd!" you say again. *"Why didn't the driver stop?"*

Who knows, but I had some theories. Maybe the driver was distracted and didn't see me in the crosswalk. One eyewitness said that she had her phone in front of her face, but there's no evidence for that, and she certainly didn't admit as much. It's the only thing that makes sense, though, given that it was a clear day and I was in the middle of the crosswalk. So, OK: she didn't see me, possibly because she was looking at her phone. That's a reasonable explanation for the initial hit. Of course, she didn't stop there.

Or, rather, she did come to a full stop for a moment, then accelerated. Why? I think the driver was trying to get away. We later learned that she had a bad-driving record and minimal insurance—only forced coverage—which meant she basically had no insurance. She must have panicked. Not great but makes some kind of sense.

But then she reversed over me. Why? I think that was a conscious decision to return to the point of impact once she realized there were witnesses and she couldn't flee the scene. Maybe she was covering her tracks.

But then what about the third time? Why did she drive forward again? I think she was confused about where I was, and maybe she was trying to get off me. The car was bouncing up and down, and maybe she got a little lost.

Maybe it finally registered for her, with all the people screaming, "Just stop driving!"

"Oh my gawd!" You lean in to whisper. *"Do you think it was a hired hit?"*

More than a few people asked if I thought my husband put a hit out on me. For the record, I'm fairly confident that Wes was not trying to off me. And if he was, then I just don't know if I should be happy or sad that he hired another bad contractor. After so many years of marriage, I thought I'd taught him better than that. So no, my husband did not put out a hit on me.

"Oh my gawd! Did she say 'sorry'?" you ask.

I'd have to take a breath when anyone asked this one. At first, I'd believed that she, like me, had been in shock, and that's why she hadn't even looked underneath her car to see if I was OK. Then maybe later her lawyer told her not to say anything. Or maybe she couldn't bring herself to, that her coping strategy was to convince herself that she wasn't at fault, or to justify her actions in some other way. I have no idea.

Saying, "No, she didn't say 'sorry,'" did not get easier, but at least the questioner's expression mirrored my own disbelief and disappointment.

"I just can't believe that," they'd say.

"Yup," I'd agree.

Sometimes my mind would stick here after the conversation had moved on. Don't all parents teach their kids to say "sorry"? I'd wonder. When you do something wrong and you get caught, aren't you supposed to say "sorry"? I mean, ideally you own up to doing something wrong and say "sorry" even if you don't get caught. That's how I was brought up, and that's how I've brought up my kids. It's just Life 101.

"Oh my gawd!" you say again. *"Was she punished?"*

Gulp. This was the toughest question to answer. Still is. Usually, I'd try to respond with something positive like "I'm focusing on my recovery, rather than the driver," or "I feel so lucky to have survived, and I try not to worry about her."
    Both of those answers were true, yet also not. Because I did worry about her, and my thoughts did turn toward her despite my efforts to focus elsewhere. That first day in traffic court, when her lawyer told her not to worry and promised to get her out of it, had broken my heart, made me question my worldview, my assumption that people were fundamentally good, that people generally wanted to do good.
    The truth? No, she was not punished, not really. But I'll get to that.

There were so many more questions. And not enough good answers. I tried my best to fill the gaps, yet the story always left people in disbelief and unsettled by the driver's behavior.

At the end of each day those first couple of months, I'd get home from work and collapse. I was no beautiful Japanese vase with golden seams. I had nothing left for my husband or my kids, not even enough energy to sit down with them for Chinese takeout or pizza. I'd just walk in the door, drop my bag, kick off my stupid flats, throw on baggy sweats and a tank top, and crawl into bed, where I stayed until morning. If I had energy, I would turn on the heating pad for my back before my eyes closed. No way did I have energy for my physical therapy exercises—sorry, Dave. My once bustling, loud house became as silent as a monastery. There were no more impromptu dance parties, no cozying up on the couch with the boys and a bowl of buttered popcorn to watch *SpongeBob SquarePants* or *iCarly*. Everyone tiptoed; everyone whispered. "Don't wake Mom" became the family mantra.

My life had been cut cleanly in two, into "before" and "after." (This, I'd learn later, was a common way for people to think about their traumatic experiences.) I was desperate to get my "before" powers back. By August, I was able to climb the stairs in my house, take a shower by myself, and get myself to the salon. I finally acknowledged that staying awake all day was too strenuous for my body and mind, so I started reserving a conference room where I would go to lay my head down for twenty or thirty minutes in the middle of the day.

One day I told my boss that, as much as I wanted to, I could no longer attend our sales kickoffs and conferences because the noise and the crowds overwhelmed me.

"No problem," he said. "You do what you need to do to get better." Just like that.

You see, something remarkable happened when I admitted that I had a disability and that I needed some accommodations—people didn't blink an eye. My colleagues were so kind, bringing me coffee or grabbing lunch for me so I wouldn't have to negotiate Manhattan's busy streets. (I'd started taking the bus into the city instead of the train, so that I wouldn't have to cross the street in the morning. The 107 Express pretty much stopped right at Microsoft's front door.) They surprised me by their easy acceptance, and I realized that, when they asked me if I was "100 percent," they weren't necessarily implying anything, or insinuating that I'd better be 100 percent or what the hell was I doing there. It was just an expression, with a lot more genuine curiosity behind it than anything else. Clearly, I was not 100 percent, and my colleagues surprised me by showing, over and over, that that was OK. The pressure to be the powerhouse I'd been before was self-imposed.

By September, I could open my eyes all the way, and I started to recover my ability to use my right arm, do minimal household chores, and, most importantly, cuddle with the kids without physical discomfort. Around that time, I accepted that just ignoring the pain wouldn't make it go away. The breast imaging, I couldn't yet face—that essential care and the mystery of my mismatched bust, I put way down on the to-do list. I wasn't ready to know.

As my mood evened out and my energy improved, I realized that it was time to follow through on the promise I'd made while trapped underneath that car. Yes, I'd decided in that moment, as blood pooled on the concrete, my family did know who I was and what I felt about things, how much I loved them. But I'd regretted not writing it down, not leaving them with something to turn to, a piece of my heart to hold in their hands when I'm gone. I'd survived this accident, but every single moment is precious; every breath is a gift, and maybe tomorrow I wouldn't be so lucky. Somehow, I needed to start paying it forward, just like the nurses said.

One lazy Sunday afternoon, when Wes and the kids were at a soccer game and the au pair was out enjoying being young and free in New York City, I sat down to put my heart on paper.

I hadn't grown up with effusive words of warmth and love—like so many things, my family just didn't talk about it. Saying "I love you" so casually was a modern American fashion that they didn't adopt. Zahid and I knew that our parents loved us, but we hadn't heard those words growing up.

That wasn't going to be my kids' experience, though. I took a sip of sparkling water, tested several different black pens, and gathered my thoughts. What did I need my kids to know?

"*Asha, Jasper, and Kalyan,*" I wrote.

The three of you are the most amazing part of my life and my deepest and most fulfilling sense of joy. If there is ever a moment in your life when I am not a phone call away, please know this:

1. You are deeply loved. Each moment of each day you are cherished, missed, and adored. Don't ever doubt the love of your family and your worth to the world.

2. You will not enjoy every moment of every day. There will be heartache and sadness and unbearable pain. We never know what triggers those moments; however, I know with absolute certainty that those moments will pass. You will always find peace, happiness, overwhelming joy, and success—if you believe in it. You must expect and strive for the best in life. Realize the tough moments provide the opportunity to use your strength, courage, and resilience to find joy again. Only you can control your thoughts—so remember how much you are loved and that a low only makes the high higher.

3. Know that you cannot change the world without effort. The kindness in all of your souls makes the sun shine brighter on the people you meet and the lives that you touch. Every time you smile, you hold a door, show a gesture of goodwill—you make the world better. Keep being honest, respectful, bucket-filling people, and enjoy the richness of that giving. It makes me so proud to see how authentically generous you three are.

You guys are amazing. I love you very much. Wherever I am, you are my joy. My joie de vivre, now and forever.

I love you always,
Mom

I left the letter on the counter for my children that evening. But guess what? They knew I loved them. So much so that they didn't seem all that interested in reading it. Now it sits in a folder in a drawer in the kitchen, should they ever feel like reading it or if, heaven forbid, something happens to me. My love for them is there, written down, just in case. My kids may not have cared at the time, but I was relieved to have written it.

Writing that love letter had opened something in me, and now I just wanted to connect even more. Surprisingly, it didn't take much work to forge deeper, more intimate, and rewarding relationships with my neighbors, fellow parents, and even my close friends like Robin and Maria. I would soon find people were hungry for connection, that they wanted honesty and authenticity, that everyone had their own secret shame that, when exposed to the light, wasn't really so bad.

CHAPTER 9

UNBREAKABLE

I've never met a strong person with an easy past.

—Unknown

As I started to reemerge into life, recounting the details of the accident became less painful. I could easily talk about the specifics of the incident—being hit and then run over three times, with the wheels going over me five times. Those nuggets did indeed make a great cocktail-party story, not that I was going to many cocktail parties yet. Crowds, even small ones, and multiple sources of sound still wore me out. But I began to get together with a few friends at a time and attend my kids' activities, an easier feat when they were outside. Of course, people wanted to know how I was doing and to hear from the source what had actually happened. We'd have that conversation I described earlier. The basic facts, the where and when and what, were easy to tell and retell, without getting emotional. What continued to be difficult was talking about the recovery, how slow and painful it was, how the vision I had of myself as a strong, unflappable woman who could think her way out of every problem had been so easily shaken.

A couple of weeks into my honesty streak, I was chatting with my hairstylist. I was telling her the short version of my cocktail-party story and mentioned how wonderful the kids had been in taking care of me. "At first, they were afraid, and they didn't understand what was going on with me. But eventually I was able to talk about it, and they really stepped up," I told her. "They'd always wanted to help me; they just hadn't known how."

She threw her arms around me and burst into tears. "Thank you," she said after a moment. "Thank you for letting your kids help you. When my mother had cancer, she never talked about it and never let us help her. I always wished that she had." I was so surprised and appreciative of her reaction; maybe sharing details of my story could help in more ways than I imagined.

My recovery continued to progress. The issues that were going to resolve themselves—walking up the stairs in our house, opening my eyes, taking a shower unaided, staying up past 9:00 p.m., going to the hair salon—already had. The issues that remained, well, I had to face the possibility that they might never vanish completely. Every now and then, I could even say them out loud: "traumatic brain injury" and "post-traumatic stress disorder." More often, though, I'd choose to focus on the day-to-day impacts and how to not only adjust my environment and behaviors but my expectations. No more listening to loud music or music in multiple rooms, riding road bikes with the kids, living without antidepressants or antianxiety medication, wearing my beloved power heels. You have no idea how much I missed those shoes.

In April 2019, we went on our first big family vacation since the accident eleven months earlier. Wes never complained about our new tame lifestyle, but I'm sure that he, too, had been feeling the constraints on his natural need for adventure. I'm sure he missed the wife who, previously, had been just as ready to do whatever to make life fun.

Usually, we would pick a tropical beach in the Caribbean or Central America; however, that was still off-limits for me. I had too many scars to chance days in the hot sun and permanent discoloration. So we decided on Europe. The kids had loved Spain and England, trips we had taken the year before the accident. A trip to Portugal would go a long way toward making my kids feel like some if not total normalcy had returned.

I was able to get around well enough, and people no longer stared at me as I walked down the sidewalk. The scars on my face had faded, and I'd left my sparkly liquid gold glitter at home (even though I still had many cracks and golden seams keeping me together). We walked the streets of Lisbon, crossed the bridges over the River Douro in Porto, and climbed the ancient city walls in Óbidos. We ate everything in sight, including those little egg puff pastries called pasteis de nata, gooey queijo de azeitao, and, of course, our favorite family vacation vegetable: ice cream—although there it was gelato. Wes and I enjoyed a shot or two of Morello cherry ginjinha, savoring that one-of-a-kind tartness. The boys were ecstatic when I surprised them with tickets to a football (soccer) game, and Asha was thrilled simply because we had sunshine and shopping.

It was adventure and laughter and beautiful family time . . . well, mostly. There was one thing that put a damper on the trip. The rules of the road in Portugal seemed to be taken as suggestions, and most of the streets were built long before cars were a thing. If I was anxious in the US, where I knew the rules and spoke the language and where we Americans sometimes take our lawsuits a little too seriously, in Portugal, I felt like being mowed down by a little two-door Renault Clio or subcompact Peugeot was not just likely but imminent. Somehow, for the locals, the dance to cross the street seemed very natural. They didn't need the cars to stop before they walked into the road; they trusted each other's steps.

I'll tell you what; I was not so trusting. I needed cars to stop completely and totally as our eyes locked in agreement before I took a step. (My therapist Linda had suggested this "active" form of communication to help me with street crossings, and I'd adopted it like a cardinal rule.) My family tried to be patient, but every now and then they'd forget, with fun parent Wes leading the charge. "Go!" he'd shout, and he and the kids would race across the street, leaving me biting my lip on the sidewalk. One beautiful evening, we were at a little plaza in Lisbon, surrounded by cute shops and restaurants. Wes, Asha, and Jasper had gone on ahead, leaving Kaly behind with me. "Let's go, Mom," he said.

I looked to the left. No cars. I looked to the right. No

cars. I looked to the left again. Still no cars. "We can't," I said.

"What do you mean?" Kaly asked, seeing what I was seeing: an empty road, with about a million tourists and locals who didn't seem to think twice about crossing, crosswalk or no, zooming traffic or no.

"Just wait, OK?" I could see him getting frustrated. I was frustrated, too, with myself.

I was aware of what was happening, of how irrational my reaction was, and yet try as I might, I could not think my way out of it.

Traumatic brain injury, I thought, admitting my vulnerability. Post-traumatic stress disorder. Then I shook my head as though shaking off a pesky fly, took Kaly's hand, exhaled, sent up a prayer, and crossed the street.

Back at home in South Orange, I was sitting on the sideline of Jasper's soccer game when a fellow mom—let's call her Wendy—asked about my recovery. I was focused on the game, and enjoying the clean morning scent of spring and freshly cut grass. I started to answer on autopilot.

"My body is healing up OK," I told her. "But I'm still struggling with post-traumatic stress disorder." I'd become much less embarrassed by this admission, although it turned out that I didn't know exactly what PTSD was. Even though it was diagnosed by Linda and my doctor, I still assumed that it was "all in my head" and that all I needed was time and a positive attitude to get over the panic attacks. I was still afraid—terrified even, active communication notwithstanding—to cross the street, and there was still a part of me that felt weak for not being "over" the accident.

Physical limitations were still so much easier for me to accept.

"Oh," said Wendy, "I have PTSD too." What? Now my focus turned to her.

"You do?" I asked. Wendy was a go-getter like me, a successful working mother who always seemed put together. Her eyeliner was always a perfect crisp line, her hair was always shiny and in place, her friendliness and positive attitude were always front and center. I'd always admired her, always been attracted to her strength. Never would I have guessed that she struggled with PTSD.

I realized, in that moment, that I didn't really know this person, that I'd taken appearances at face value and assumed, given her crisp eyeliner, that she had it together outside and in.

"Yup. It's something I've been dealing with for a long time."

"Really?" I still couldn't quite believe it.

She laughed. "Yes, really. There's some stuff from my childhood that I never fully looked at."

A dad two rows down shouted, "What kind of call was that, ref? Did you not see that kid's elbow?"

Wendy and I smiled at each other. "I actually just left my job so I could focus on it," she went on. "It's been impacting my life for so long, and I got tired of grinning and bearing it. I finally had to admit to myself that it's not going to go away on its own. I can't just think my way out of it."

A light bulb went on. I can't just think my way out of it.

"That's what I've been trying to tell you!" said Linda when I mentioned this conversation to her.

I guess I hadn't been listening or hadn't integrated the thing I didn't want to hear. Now I was determined to catch up. Linda recommended Bessel A. Van der Kolk's *The Body Keeps the Score: Brain, Mind, and Body in the Healing of Trauma*, and I ordered my copy that afternoon.

Before the accident, I'd been reading books with titles like *The Achievement Habit* by Bernard Roth and *Extreme Ownership: How U.S. Navy SEALs Lead* and *Win* by Jocko Willink, with sentiments like "Leaders must own everything in their world. There is no one else to blame."

Yes! I'd think. I am the boss of me, the boss of my destiny.

I still believed that, but with some amendments.

It had been a long time since I'd cracked a book. Since May 21, 2018, if you're asking. I just couldn't focus my mind long enough to follow a chapter-length thread, and I couldn't focus my eyes very long without pain. Instead, I'd relied on snippets of wisdom, quotes I'd find online. I would screenshot them so I could find a jolt of inspiration when life felt heavy, when I needed a mini pep talk. You may have noticed many of these at the beginning of each chapter.

Now, however, I was ready to take on a book again. I gobbled up *The Body Keeps the Score*, or, rather, I nibbled at it slowly, since my book-gobbling days were behind me. There is almost nothing better than reading a book and finding out that all those haunting questions and doubts and fears that felt so personal, so shameful and isolating, were actually pretty standard. Lots of people experience trauma, and lots of people experience post-traumatic stress disorder. I wasn't alone, and what happened to me and what was still happening to me were not some unique and evil curse; they were just things that happen to animals living in the world. As normal and natural as any other kind of cause and effect.

"Trauma results in a fundamental reorganization of the way mind and brain manage perceptions," the author writes. "It changes not only how we think and what we think about, but also our very capacity to think." I had to put the book down and close my eyes when I read that. For the first time in forever, I felt like I could breathe, really breathe. My heart slowed into a regular beat.

Turns out that PTSD is psychological, physical, physiological. My inability to mentally navigate my way through it did not, in fact, mean that I was weak-minded, or weak in general. All the things I had been telling myself—consciously or not—weren't true. I wasn't dumb; I wasn't a failure, a disappointment, a downer. I shouldn't "know better." PTSD was not something to "conquer." It was something that happens with trauma, and that's OK. Not fun, not pleasant, but OK. Maybe I could let myself off the hook.

After that, I started paying more attention to my sensations rather than denying them or beating myself up over them. I'm feeling panicky, I'd think to myself before crossing the street. My chest is tight; my legs feel shaky. And that's OK.

Soon after, in early May 2019, I found myself at a car dealership, planning to trade in our little, and very old, Prius. I just got too anxious when behind the wheel of our small cars, and so I decided that maybe it was time for an upgrade, at least size wise. I was perusing a row of one-year-old Land Rover Discoveries in the lot when my eye caught on an older Mercedes G-Class, a boxy beast of an SUV. I walked over.

"What about this one?" I asked the dealer.

He checked the listing. "It's ten years old . . . ," he said, raising an eyebrow.

"Can I test-drive it?"

My entire body relaxed when I got in the driver's seat of that tank. For what it lacked in the most up-to-date luxury features—no Apple CarPlay or blind-spot warnings or even multiple cup holders—it made up for in sheer solidity. I called Wes.

"Did you just say it's ten years old?" he asked.

"Yes. But I feel fabulous."

We bought the car and, with it, the comfort of safety, of confidence, of badass-ness that I had forgotten I could possess. "I feel so good in that car," I later told Linda. "It's like I am me again."

"When's the last time you felt like that?" she asked, smiling, clearly happy for me.

I thought about it, going back over the last days and weeks and months. "The day of the accident," I finally said.

Later that same week, Westcott, some close friends, and I went to a Basquiat exhibit at the Brant Foundation in Lower Manhattan. We were all Basquiat fans, and since this was an exhibit with timed entries and the building had huge rooms and high ceilings, I didn't need to worry about a swarm of noisy crowds or overstimulation. Just my speed! As we were walking around, we were discussing the upcoming first anniversary of the accident. We knew we wanted to celebrate the day—but we struggled with how to say that, what to call our special day, our new holiday. Everyone had been calling me unbreakable since no bones were broken—however, I worried that calling myself "unbreakable" would make me sound boastful.

At the same time, though, I was letting myself off the hook a bit by understanding PTSD. I was finding a little mojo behind the wheel of my new tank. And here I was now, enjoying Basquiat's vibrant paintings. There, in the middle of the exhibit, I told my friends that I finally remembered what it felt like to be happy and strong. That I had been feeling happy for a while, but strength was much more elusive. We all knew life was different now, but it wasn't broken anymore. I had finally earned my golden seams. We all had something to celebrate. And just as I said that, we came to a painting I hadn't seen before. It was a striking piece full of energy with its bold colors and ambiguous shapes. The word Unbreakable ran across it. We all looked at each other and knew. That was it. Our holiday would be called Unbreakable Day.

Wes, the kids, and I celebrated that first year with just a simple family dinner and a long email thanking the people we loved and who helped us reach this point, including my mom and dad, Zahid, the kids, Maria, Robin, and my medical team of heroes: my doctor, Linda, and Dave. I also shared a few of the lessons, insights I had gained over the past year. I sent the email to everyone who had played a role—big or small—in my journey since the accident. It was a "blast" of communication I wasn't used to making, but it was the start of my efforts to pay it forward and to share with vulnerability and gratitude.

Two months later, in late July, I was sitting in the backyard of a casual friend; let's call her Kelly. Usually, we'd be hanging out with other couples, but tonight it was just the four of us. Kelly had a slightly quirky personality, and she'd say stuff like "No one likes me, but fortunately they like my husband."

This husband and Wes were inside, prepping the meat

and veggies for the grill while we relaxed, sipping chilled Chardonnay and eating too many crackers with cheese— well, I was eating too many crackers and cheese. She asked me about the accident, as people in the community tended to do; even after all these months, it was still a good cocktail-party story. I gave her the synopsis, which she already mostly knew. She asked the usual questions; I gave my usual answers. At that point, the healing process was more interesting, at least to me, than the accident itself, and so I talked some about my new insight into PTSD, and how I was working to accept the new version of me, and how my kids had been so wonderful during this hard time.

Eventually, we got to reminiscing about when our kids were young, about art projects and school pickups. "You know," she said, leaning back in her chaise with her wine, "I really didn't like you much before."

Record scratch.

I swallowed. Very creative phrasing, I thought. "What do you mean?" I asked.

"You were always so put together. You've got this good job, and such nice kids, and you always looked good. You were really an unsympathetic character."

Part of me was perplexed. Apparently, she had done what I had done to Wendy at the soccer game, but where my assumptions had brought on admiration, Kelly's assumptions had led her down a different path. Thing was, she didn't really know me, just as I hadn't really known Wendy. Now, I didn't quite know what to say, so I tried to laugh it off. "Well," I said, "I'm glad you like me now!"

Another part of me really appreciated the fact that Kelly felt comfortable enough to say that to me. Here she was, being honest and authentic with me, in her particular, blunt way. This seemed like a sign that my attempts to be more vulnerable, to be real, were succeeding. I was no longer trying so hard to be the powerhouse I'd been, or to pretend that eventually I would be her again—or even that I wanted to be. I was done with that. Now I could just be me, cracks and gold glitter and all. And maybe that meant that the people around me could just be themselves too.

SORRY, NOT SORRY

Better to be the one who smiled than the
one who didn't smile back.
—Mari Gayatri Stein

Here's where things get messy. Again.

Twenty-one months after the accident, Westcott and
I were deposed by our insurance company. Because the
driver only had "forced coverage," we'd had to seek pay-
ments from our own auto insurer, and we were still wran-
gling with them about my medical bills. This was another
ongoing struggle, another daily stressor, alongside the actual recovery process. Luckily, we had hired a law firm to
help us. At first, I was very against it, as I worried being
litigious would make me seem vindictive, unforgiving, or
money hungry. I didn't want that negative energy. Luckily,
my worries were unfounded. The experience showed me
just how important it is to have knowledgeable people

on our side. In fact, I am not sure we would have made it through the years and mountains of bills, paperwork, and difficult conversations, like this one, without them.

It was February 11, 2020, a cold, slushy day with cement-colored clouds sitting low in the sky. On the radio, journalists were talking about a strange new flu in China, about vague, conflicting reports coming out of Wuhan. The kids were in school, the au pair taking care of drop-offs and pickups.

I did not expect to see the driver that day. She probably looked at me and thought I was fine. I was dressed in my business casual winter uniform—dark blue fitted flare jeans, sturdy block-heeled boots, and a black cashmere turtleneck. I put on a blazer that day too—something about a lawyer's office made me feel like I needed to emphasize the "business" in "business casual." I looked "normal," and I could stand up tall and straight again—no cane these days—yet as soon as I saw her, my stiff back collapsed, and I could barely take another step forward. Her back was to the door, her posture slumped, protective. Westcott and I exchanged a look. From this angle, she didn't seem so big and mean and terrible. I cleared my throat, took a deep breath, and steeled myself for what I knew I had to do: behave like a grown-up.

"Hello," I said, going around the room to the insurance company lawyers, the court transcriber, the paralegals, introducing myself and shaking hands. I wanted these people to see my face, to see that I was an actual person, to bring a little humanity to the proceedings, a process that, most of the time, just felt cold. How many hours had Westcott or I spent on the phone, trying to communicate the basics of the injury, and why we had so many medical bills, and why it was our insurer's duty to pay them? How many hours had we spent on hold, listening to some godawful Muzak periodically interrupted by a voice saying that the call was important to them?

Now, I wanted to look around at everyone and say, Hello! Real person run over by car here! Lots of pain! Lots of anguish! Just trying to get my life back!

Finally, I made it to the driver and her lawyer. She still looked unassuming, a bit nervous, practically swallowed up by the big comfy corporate chair. This woman is not her mistake, I reminded myself. I took a breath and discreetly wiped my suddenly clammy hands on my casual blazer. A glimmer of hope flashed in my chest. Now was a chance for us to have our moment, to make some kind of basic human connection, to see eye to eye. Maybe she couldn't say the actual words "I'm sorry," but all it would take was a look, a pause, a tiny extra pressure when she shook my hand for me to see it as a sign of acknowledgment, even remorse. I'd forget all about that day in court, about that lawyer saying, "Don't worry. We'll get you out of this." I knew that I was grabbing at straws here, not just willing but eager to accept any crumb of evidence that she cared that she'd hurt me. I'd take whatever I could get.

"Hello," I said, offering my hand. "I'm Naseem."

The driver shook my hand without looking up, her eyes glued to the mahogany conference table, her own hand dry and limp. Just like that, my hope died, like a candle going out, leaving a trail of smoke. I let go, then shook her lawyer's hand and went over to my seat, blinking hard and trying to slow my racing heart.

Things went downhill from there. It was clear from the first moment of the driver's deposition that she did not understand what was going on. Turned out, language was a barrier for her, and it seemed as though her lawyer had not gone to the trouble to explain the situation. She had been unaware that her insurance didn't cover liability, and she couldn't quite remember what kind of tickets she'd received. She'd ended up pleading guilty for failure to yield to a pedestrian and careless driving only because of the prohibitive cost of the lawyer's fees.

You may not believe me, but a part of me still felt empathy for her. Here was an immigrant, like my own parents, but with a part-time minimum-wage job, who had been thrown into the same opaque, often dehumanizing system that we, with our English fluency and master's degrees and monetary resources and lawyer friends and doctor relatives, had struggled to navigate. Whom did she have to help her?

Then again, she really, truly did not seem to care. Or, if she did, any caring was wholly eclipsed by her instinct for self-preservation. But what was she afraid of? That we'd sue her personally? It was clear where that would get us: not very far. The reason we were here was to prove to our insurance company why they had to foot the bill or, rather, reimburse us for the astronomical medical expenses we'd already paid. No matter what happened in the day's proceedings, her bank account would not feel the burn. At this point, all I wanted from her was acknowledgment, something that would make sense to me.

We'd given up trying to get that from the justice system. The week after that first time in court, I'd written a letter to the Essex County South Orange–Maplewood Municipal Court. I wanted them to understand the nature of the incident and how deeply it had impacted me and my family and remind them of their duty under the law. I'd tried to strike a balance between factual and emotional, and it had taken me a few drafts and lots of help from Wes and my friend Robin to get there. I was still in a lot of physical pain, and the callous treatment not only of the driver and her lawyer but the prosecutor and the system as a whole had piled on the pain.

Ultimately, my input didn't matter. The driver's running over me—three times, with the tires going over me five times—had essentially been treated as a minor traffic accident, with her paying the minimum fine of $200 and losing her license for only ten days—$200 and ten days!

Thanks to my recently purchased tank of an SUV, I was no longer afraid to get behind the wheel, but I wouldn't say that driving was easy. I worried that I might hit someone. I worried when I saw someone approaching the crosswalk or in the crosswalk, somehow simultaneously experiencing myself as the driver and projecting myself onto them, the pedestrian who has no idea just how vulnerable they are. What if I accidentally hit them? What if I hit them and then got confused or scared and didn't respond as I should? Not a street crossing went by that didn't make my palms sweat and send my heart rate sky high. Would I ever feel safe again?

And $200—that was a drop in the bucket compared to the salary and commissions I'd lost or the amount of time Wes could have been working but had spent taking care of me or on the phone arguing on my behalf. The kids, Jasper in particular, had started worrying about money. We'd go out to dinner, and he wouldn't order. "We're fine!" I'd tell him. He'd say, "Oh, I'm not hungry," but I knew that he was scared, that he didn't want to add to our financial burden.

I'm not a punitive or vindictive person, truly, but I do believe in . . . justice? Consequences for our actions? Karma?
The laws of cause and effect?

During her questioning, the driver talked in circles,
round and round and round. At a certain point, our lawyer said, "You got to answer the questions I ask, or we're
going to be here all day. This could take two minutes or
two hours, depending on how you answer these questions."
I had my head in my hands. This was torture, sitting there
in those big chairs, the beige carpet under our feet and the
fluorescent overhead light turning everyone sallow. Every
time she sidestepped a question about the basic facts,
that there were witnesses at the scene, that the police
had taken witness statements that put me squarely in the
crosswalk—not up the hill jaywalking, as she claimed—I
felt the vise around my chest tighten.

"She wasn't in the crosswalk," the driver told the questioner. "If they say that, it's not true."

Westcott put his hand on my back.

The driver would not concede anything, no matter the
evidence presented, no matter the lawyer's explanation of
how witness testimony and police procedure works. "They
listened to what you said because you went to the police
station and told them. They listened to what Ms. Rochette
said. They listened to what her husband said. They listened to what several other people said. They took mea-
surements. They did an investigation and found that you
struck her in the crosswalk; do you understand that?" he
asked.

"And I was by myself. I have no witnesses," she said. "I
have no one with me for my witness. That day God was my
witness."

I practically choked.

She continued. "God was there. If God wasn't there, it would have been worse."

"What wasn't going to be worse, how injured this woman—"

"Yeah, because it's—"

"Do you realize how injured this woman was?"

"It's an accident."

"You ran her over three times."

"It's an accident."

"We know it's an accident. So why can't you tell us the truth?"

I felt like I wanted to curl up and die, like I had when I was trapped underneath the car, when my entire world was four tires, asphalt, and pain. The rest of the deposition passed in a blur. I was rattled. My turn immediately followed the driver's, and as the insurance company's attorney repeated the instructions—wait for her to fully ask the questions before answering; all answers must be verbalized so that the court reporter can record them; no help from my husband; my obligation to tell the truth, and so on—I tried to collect myself. I kept my shaking hands in my lap, taking deep breaths and focusing on the immediate space, my feet on the floor, my back on the chair. Then it was my turn for questioning.

After the insurance attorney reiterated my obligation to tell the truth, she asked, "Are you under the influence of any medications, alcohol, or other substances that could affect your memory today?"

I flinched. Here we go, I thought.

"So, since the accident, I have started taking anti-anxiety and antidepressants," I said, feeling my cheeks turn red and feeling my mouth tripping over the words. "If those, you know, could cause—I don't think those cause, you know, any issue to my memory, but I just want to alert you that I'm taking those."

After that awkward opening, though, the questioning went smoothly. I stated how the accident had impacted my work, how I'd been forced to work from home more often, how it had limited my ability to travel, how much commission income I'd lost during my eight weeks of sick leave. About how much time I had to use during my workdays for doctor's appointments—thank goodness Microsoft was flexible. When the attorney asked about my cane and knee brace, I mentioned those stupid flats or boring block heels I now had to wear, how the accident significantly altered my freedom to present myself as I chose.

The diagrams of the scene came out soon thereafter, and we went over, in painful, meticulous detail, the location and timing and play-by-play of the accident. Then we looked over the day-after photos, the Frankenstein version of me that scared my children, with stitches and bruises and dried blood, my left eye swollen shut. From a week later, the purple striations on my neck and head, the pink inner flesh of my wounded knee, my stitched ear and bruised chin. The photos of my right breast were the worst: the raw, red-rimmed flesh covering up my nipple, like it wasn't even there. I knew I shouldn't be embarrassed, but I was, in front of this roomful of lawyers eyeing my exposed, though hideously injured, breast. I was different, again. Exposed and ashamed. I'd yet to return to the doctor's office for breast imaging, I remembered with a tinge of guilt, after I'd ditched the original appointment to go into the city for that doomed margarita.

I glanced over at the driver; she was staring at the table. Whether God was her witness or not, there was no denying the photographs. I'd been thoroughly mangled, and here was proof, as important to the case as it was to my own mental state, a reminder in the face of my own ongoing incredulousness and disappointment that the accident had indeed been real. Real and really serious.

The questioning continued, now focused on how the injuries had impacted my life and what medical treatments I'd needed for recovery. How my life quite literally shattered. Of course, there were no photos of the concussion—you can't see a traumatic brain injury from the outside—and so I brought up those symptoms, as well as reiterated my new diagnoses of anxiety and depression, the terror and panic attacks and irritability and overwhelm, and the sessions with Linda to address them. I talked about my excruciating physical therapy sessions with Dave. I talked about the impact on my children, how frightened they'd been and how much responsibility had suddenly fallen on my thirteen-year-old daughter's shoulders, how my family couldn't fully understand why I now freaked out when attempting to cross the street. My weight gain and wardrobe change. Again, those stupid flats. All those activities I'd taken for granted before, like kickboxing and driving longer distances and going to concerts and blow-drying my hair, had fallen out of my range.

Pause for a moment and time travel with me. It's 1999, almost twenty years earlier, on a scorching-hot day in Black Rock City. I'm wobbling on a little kid's bike, a pink-and-lavender Barbie bike with shimmery magenta tassels, on the playa at Burning Man, surrounded by tents and

RVs and blaring music and many kinds of smoke. Wes is cheering me on; he just taught me how to ride a bike! The sun is shining in my eyes; there's a coating of dust on everything; sweat is beading on my face, and I'm happy—no, thrilled—to be there, to be free in ways that my nervous parents would have never imagined.

It was a big moment when I had finally learned to ride a bike. I was so proud that I could cruise with Wes and kids. To have that taken away from me—from all of us—was devastating and so hard to accept. It was all gone. At least for now.

As the deposition continued, my husband went over the whole ordeal again for the lawyers. He was composed, though I could hear the anger just under the surface, and the fear when he talked about how he'd initially thought I was dead, then paralyzed. How the accident had affected him and the family. He didn't reveal anything I didn't already know, but still it was hard to hear.

At the end of the meeting, Wes and I went into a conference room next door with our lawyer and collapsed into the chairs around another boardroom table. Celebrating our Unbreakable Day last year seemed like a dream, a lie. I felt broken all over again.

"Can you believe that?" we asked one another, identical stunned expressions on our faces.

"Can you believe her? Can you believe she said, 'God was my witness'?"

We would not be getting any kind of acknowledgment, it seemed. She would never give us the missing piece of the puzzle by telling us how such a thing had happened or why she'd behaved as she did. There would be no human

connection, no compassion, no making sense. I'm still trying to accept this. I'm not sure I ever will.

One thing for sure, though: if I'd heard the driver say,
"I'm sorry"—just those two words—I would have been a lot
further along. Like I said, it's messy. And as I soon learned,
trauma recovery is never really "over." Trauma can open
itself up in the least expected ways.

CHAPTER

PAYING IT FORWARD

> Do not worry that your life is turning up-
> side down. How do you know that the side
> you are used to is better than the one to
> come?
>
> —Rumi

Just about a year after the accident, I had enough distance and perspective on the experience to feel good and to start taking note of what I had learned. I shared some of my early learnings in my Unbreakable Day email, and other insights were manifesting in my thoughts and actions—even subconsciously.

I was incorporating many of the life lessons into my work too. At this point, with almost twenty years of sales experience, I knew how to handle executive conversations, navigate long, complex sales cycles at Fortune 100 companies—and the accompanying politics—and I knew how to wrangle and rally the large teams needed to support such deals. It was what I had done for years, and many of those skills felt like natural habits.

After the accident, as the wiring of my brain had changed, some of those habits took more effort. Some were no longer natural, and others had evolved into a thoughtful practice and approach. To help keep me on track, I created a framework, my talk track, with some very straightforward principles. After going over it a few times, I realized that I was actually using all the same principles that helped me overcome the trauma and reshape the accident into Unbreakable Day.

Let's say you're a new client. I would start our conversation about how innovation is just some level of change. In my case, that innovation was accepting that I would never be the person I was before the trauma and letting that be OK.

I would then introduce a very simple plan change: Recognize your ambition. Ask questions. Ask why. Consciously create your story.

For me, my ambition was about using the accident to be better. To "play my game better." I didn't want to change my game—I really liked my life. I just wanted to be a better version of me. I wasn't quite sure what that meant or how I would do it at first; however, I knew that was my goal. I wanted to be better, and I wanted to pay it forward.

Once you know your goal, it's time to ask how to achieve it. Like many goals in business and life, I reached mine by taking small steps, by regularly reexamining myself, recognizing lessons and insights. Then it was doing the uncomfortable work of sharing.

I would then tell you that after you ask yourself, and

maybe your team, questions, you go back and create a vision statement. What's the reason you're making this change? For me, that vision became the Unbreakable Day. However, just having that vision, that rally cry, isn't enough. You need to frame your thinking around that success. What are the stories you are going to tell to create that vision? What are you not going to tell?

For me, the only story I was sure of was that I would look back on the accident and be better, stronger. I was going to make sure my kids didn't long for the pre-accident mom, a person I wasn't and couldn't be. I was going to share my wisdom and my experience to help others. I was going to remember how lucky I was to survive.

I wasn't going to say that I must be unlucky for getting hit by a car. I wasn't going to focus on the things I couldn't do. I wasn't going to waste time wishing I had taken a different train or had asked my husband to pick me up at the station. I was going to look back and not mind having been in a crazy, horrific accident.

And then I tried my hardest to live that way. When things didn't work, I did my best to accept, adapt, and change course. When I found going off my antidepressants wasn't an option yet, I kept taking them. When I learned that my knee might give out at any time, I started buying more flats (and more block heels). When I reflected on my accident, I often thought, How cool is it that I survived being hit and then run over three times?

My process was working. I was transforming. I was feeling good.

And then, the pandemic hit. You know what happened next. Everything ground to a halt. We watched the news, wondering if the novel virus would reach us in America, how much danger we were really in. We stocked up on toilet paper and sheltered in place, wondering how long it would last. We bought lots of face masks and hand sanitizer by the gallon, wondering when things would go back to normal. The kids started virtual school, and I had to turn my camera on for every meeting, which was the only way to see people. I could no longer be upset about having to wear my stupid flats, when the new global uniform was sweatpants and slippers. (Although I actually never succumbed to the sweatpants. Even my Zoom days started with extralarge gold hoops and some variation of honeysuckle or jasmine perfume.)

While we settled in at home, hospitals were overrun and, for a while, appointments unrelated to COVID-19 were canceled to make room for the infected. People got sick and recovered; people got sick and died. Fear and anxiety and shock and overwhelm and grief were everywhere. The new normal. A global, seemingly never-ending Unbreakable Day. (That was when I knew it was time for me to write down the story you hold in your hands. I wanted to pay it forward.)

Being at home also gave some reprieve from my panic attacks. I didn't have to walk across busy streets anymore. However, I did eventually have to go out and revisit my issues. Once doctors' offices were reopened, I steeled myself and finally went in for breast imaging. As feared, surgery was called for, and when the surgeon went in to repair my breasts, he found that my pectoral muscle was torn and flattened to the exact width of a tire. He said he had never seen anything like it. As much as this discovery horrified me, it also brought me comfort. Yes, a car had hit me, then reversed, then drove over me again. Yes, tires had really run over my head, chest, and knees. I was not imagining it. Here was proof. This was another way my trauma resurfaced. The denial cycled back over and over. You'd think I would no longer need validation, but I did. I still do. Even though my husband was right there and saw the whole thing, even though there were witnesses who gave consistent accounts to the police, though I have photos of my injuries and records of my medical and physical therapy with Dave, my trauma therapy appointments with Linda, though I have a cane I no longer need sitting in the back of the closet and a tube of gold glitter at the bottom of my makeup case—it's still surreal. Even though our insurance company finally, after almost three years, paid out a settlement. Even though all that evidence is there, the accident was so bizarre that it defies belief, a fact I'm reminded of every time I tell the story.

"Wait, what?" everyone always says.

My daughter's school counselor even advised against giving details of the accident in her college essay—worried admissions officers would think Asha was lying. Wild, right?

I still have to actively keep from fretting about the driver. When people ask us about her now, I try to focus on how happy I am to be alive. If I let my mind go too far into the weeds, I will still spin out. Her lack of remorse, accountability, and, at the end of the day, basic human kindness was a crime far worse than hitting me or driving over me. Mistakes happen—that's life. It's the not saying "sorry" that keeps the wounds open.

I remind myself, over and over and over, that it wasn't personal. The driver was certainly not out to get me, and more than likely, her actions following the accident were tied to a set of circumstances that I know nothing about nor could ever imagine. I'd like to think we all try to behave according to some shared moral code, but the world is just too big, and it treats each of us so differently, that maybe that assumption is naive. What she did was not out of malice—there was something else going on that I'll never know. Whatever that was, it wasn't personal.

Of course, I forget my wisdom sometimes. It's really, really hard to remember that epiphany I had last week about acceptance or forgiveness when, this week, my back hurts again or I feel panicky about crossing the street. Trauma recovery is not linear—it's a process of remembering and forgetting, remembering and forgetting. But I want to remember more often than not. So I got some permanent cues to help me.

I got tattoos. The first is the phrase joie de vivre next to three stars, one for each of my children, a reminder that life is joy, and I am so thankful to be alive, and that in those moments under the car, thoughts of Asha, Jasper, and Kaly brought me strength and happiness. The second is a dandelion in that seed puffball phase. It's a reminder of that moment in the park when I slowed down, a reminder to not let the twists and turns of my journey keep me from enjoying the simple pleasures of the world around me. The third is the Japanese phrase ichi-go ichi-e, which roughly means that the moment we are experiencing will never happen again. It's about treasuring the unrepeatable nature of a moment and recognizing that who we are in the moment, we will never be again. We are constantly transforming, over and over.

This last tattoo was especially meaningful for me in

late 2021 and early 2022, when I found myself wondering if I had taken my own advice and fully appreciated the people I loved.

My parents died within weeks of each other at the end of 2021. Zahid and I went from having loving parents who adored us, and whom we counted on—and maybe even took for granted—to all of a sudden being orphans. In an instant, I no longer had the security of my dad, a man whom I knew loved me more than anyone in the world ever would. And my mom had been instrumental in my becoming the strong, spontaneous woman I like to think I am. (Hello, tattoos!) She had been ill for years, but she was still there for me to ask questions and share victories. I was unprepared for the searing pain of this loss.

My dad had called at the beginning of November, in his usual chipper mood.

"Hi, Nas!" he said. "How are you?" As always, I could hear his bright smile through the phone. We went on chatting until he casually mentioned that he wasn't feeling so great. "But," he quickly added, "it's probably just nothing."

I looked at the clock. It was a Friday afternoon, and I had a busy evening ahead of me. But it wasn't really that late, and my dad so rarely complained that I thought I'd better pay attention. "How about I come over for an hour?" I said. "We can go to urgent care if we need to."

Zahid was in town, in the process of moving back after thirty-five years in California, and I picked him up on the way. It was so wonderful having him around, and we'd long since moved on from our professional venture together. He wanted to be near family again, and we were so excited about the future, all of us having brunch together on Sundays and sharing holidays and getting to see each other whenever. My dad could never get enough of family time—if we went there for an hour, he wanted to know why we weren't there for two!

A few minutes after Zahid got in the car, my dad called back. "It's probably just indigestion," he said. "You don't need to come."

Screw that downplay; we went anyway. My dad was in great health. We had no reason to worry at that moment; still, I could tell that something wasn't right. As soon as we walked in the door, I realized it might be worse than I thought, as my dad was still in his bathrobe! For my entire life, I had never seen my dad in a bathrobe after 7:00 a.m. And it was four o'clock in the afternoon! He greeted us with a big smile as always, but his color was off. There was pain behind his jovial smile.

"Come on, Dad," I gently urged. "Why don't you take a COVID-19 test, and then we'll go to urgent care? If it turns out to be nothing, then no big deal."

It took some doing to convince him—doctors really are the worst patients—but finally we got him up and ready to go. My mom stayed behind. If my dad was in trouble, we couldn't afford the time it would take to get her in the car and load up her wheelchair; plus they had an amazing caregiver who was there for the evening shift, so my dad was at ease knowing she would be OK. "I'll be back soon," he said to her as he put on his coat. "Don't worry, Sena."

At urgent care, my dad told the triage nurse about his pain and was moved to the front of the line. Soon after he went back to an exam room, a doctor came out the swinging doors and approached. "You are Dr. Hussain's family?" she asked. Zahid and I stood up. "Your dad is having a heart attack. We need to take him to the emergency room in Trenton."

A nurse wheeled my dad out to the ambulance loading zone, and I immediately did what I did the day of my accident: I tried to negotiate with the medics about taking him to the most luxurious hospital in the area.

"That's not how this works, ma'am," one of them politely told me. "We need to take him to the Cardiac Trauma Center. He can't just go anywhere."

My dad, brother, and I exchanged looks. Did he really need to go to Cardiac Trauma? Couldn't he go to the nicer hospital nearby? Even as they were strapping him in, my dad still refused to believe he was having a heart attack. "It's just indigestion!" he said. "Take me home!" He was a retired hematologist-oncologist, a man who'd gotten used to having his orders followed. But this time, no one listened.

It was a heart attack. Three of his arteries were clogged, and he was put on the schedule for a triple bypass a few days out. He was staying at the hospital for at least the week (and it was a week that would be oddly relaxing for my dad).

I canceled my Friday evening plans, and then Zahid and I moved in with my mom. We would now need to take care of her—that was not relaxing. Luckily, Wes could be home with the kids (we didn't have an au pair anymore), and so that was one less thing for me to worry about.

My brother and I were not too far from my dad's hospital and could go visit him every morning and afternoon when the caregivers could take over with my mom. Just as when Jasper broke his arm, we got a chance to sit around the hospital room and talk and tell stories. My dad was in a great mood. Though he never said it, I think that he was glad to get a break from his responsibilities caring for my mom. Who could blame him? He'd been her primary caregiver for more than a dozen years. He never complained; he was always attentive and gentle, but that amount of work must wear on a person, on top of the distress of seeing someone they love suffer and, over time, lose their most basic abilities. It certainly wore on my brother and me after only a few weeks; I have no idea how my dad had the strength to do it for years.

I squeezed his hand the morning of the surgery, before the nurses kicked us out so they could prep him. "You're going to be fine, Dad," I said confidently.

Three hours turned into five hours turned into eight hours. The triple bypass turned into a quintuple bypass.

When we were finally allowed in, I walked into the recovery room with only a little bit of trepidation. Seeing him lying there under the thin hospital blanket, tubes attached to him everywhere, was jarring. I thought of my own kids when they entered my hospital room after the accident. Brave Asha. Kaly hiding behind her. Jasper, bursting into tears. Now here was my dad, a man who never stopped moving, never stopped being the host of the party. "Hi, Dad," I said softly.

He opened his eyes and looked around groggily, then closed them again. This went on for days. "It's too hard," he whispered.

Those three words became his mantra.

I was surprised, saddened, frustrated, and even angry. He'd been taking care of my mom for years and, before that, taking care of thousands of patients for decades. Now that he was the patient, it was too hard? Had the isolation of COVID-19 made him this depressed? Where was the hope he gave everyone else? (And if I couldn't convince my dad to find hope, how could I share my story and expect to help a stranger?)

Then again, I could relate. I'd had my own moment of giving up when the car had driven over my head and neck. I'd felt so tired, and I'd accepted what I believed to be my fate. I'd let go. But even if, in that moment, I was done with the world, the world wasn't done with me. So I assumed that my dad was just having his white-flag moment, and he'd soon feel better and move on.

I still don't really understand what happened. He was a different person after his surgery, one without hope. I don't know if it was the pain, or if a building exhaustion and lone-liness had finally caught up with him, or if he no longer had the motivation to maintain his smiling stoicism. A three-, then four-day stint became a month. We briefly got a taste of hope when the hospital told me that he was almost ready for rehab. He left the ICU for only one day before his blood pressure dived and he had to be sedated and put on a ventilator back in the ICU. I never heard his voice again. Ten days later, he was gone. I think my dad didn't have a story of hope when he went into this crisis. He didn't think about who he wanted to be after something so tough. He didn't see past his long, exhausting battle in the hospital, and he knew my mom couldn't fight much longer.

When I went into my crisis, my life was happy. I'd fed myself countless inspirational stories about persever-ance. I always told myself that I would be that person who wouldn't give up, who would come out the other side of anything. For me, that other side also included a wonderful happy life that was social and vibrant and full—a life that my dad hadn't enjoyed since lockdown started and maybe even before that, given my mom's health issues. His life those last few years had been hard. Very hard.

For the six weeks my dad was in the hospital, my mom waited anxiously at home. She hadn't been able to see him at the hospital because of COVID-19 protocol and her own health. Their sixtieth anniversary was coming up, and those weeks were the longest time they'd ever been apart.

The morning he died, she said, "We're not making any decisions today."

"Yes," I said. "We're not making any decisions today. Today we're just accepting."

Then my mom died a few weeks later. When my dad died, she knew her story was over.

I was, and still am, heartbroken. I can't say that my other hardships in any way prepared me for this. In my experience, loss—life—doesn't work like that. It hurts, every time, in a new yet familiar way. There are tools that we may acquire through experience: facing our feelings, talking with friends and family and professionals, snatching moments of joy or pleasure amidst pain. Recognizing that grief is nebulous and ever-changing, that yesterday it was one thing and tomorrow it will be something else entirely. We will always face new challenges, as long as we live. But I guess that's life in a nutshell, isn't it?

What I can say is that previous losses reveal the capacity to survive, and hopefully we can remember that capacity during the next loss or crisis. And it helps to have a story of hope that's strong enough to survive as well. A story made of snapshots of joy: eating ice cream with my kids on a foreign street; finally learning how to ride a bike in the middle of a hot desert playa; snorkeling in a sparkling blue sea; cozying up on the couch after soccer practice.

There has to be something we can cling to in the darkest nights of grief, something to keep us tethered to life, even if it's just a glimmer of a memory that we've been there before and we got through it, that this state and all states of being are not forever. Life goes on.

Less than two months after my parents died, my dear friend Maria lost her teenage son. He was handsome, brilliant, and adored by his family and friends. He died by suicide. There are no words to describe this, or at least no words that belong to me. It's not my story to tell.

When I got the news, I did two things. First, I broke down. I cried. I screamed. I hyperventilated. I ached because my person—my confidante and soul sister of twenty-five years—was facing a horrific and heartbreaking loss. And also because I was terrified that my friend was gone. I had just lost my parents; I couldn't handle losing Maria too. It was such a selfish thought. I feel guilty and even ashamed about it, but that's how much I love her and need her in my life. Second, I pulled myself together and did the only thing I could for her: I showed up. She told me not to come, but I knew very well from experience that sometimes the thing we need is something we can't ask for.

Death was a fresh experience for me, and I knew how uncomfortable people are around it. Death in general is tough, and death of a child and death by suicide—even tougher. The horror of it is incomprehensible, beyond overwhelming. But not talking about it or not showing up is not going to make it go away. I knew that with certainty.

So· we talked about it. Only when she wanted to. I didn't ask questions; I didn't ask how she was. Questions, I'd learned, even with good intentions, are just too hard when you're in the middle of unbearable trauma. We also spent a lot of time sitting together in silence, crying, and even laughing in those moments when we could distract ourselves. I'd also learned that wallowing in pain brings no relief. It's OK to be kind to yourself, to let yourself find a moment of joy even in darkness.

One morning after holding Maria's hand and wishing I could take away her pain for just one second, I realized that, for all my efforts to be a more honest, open person, to share my story so that other people would feel like they could share theirs, I'd still been holding back.

I'm not sure whether I'd kept this one thing to myself for decades because I was ashamed, or whether it had become such a distant memory that it had lost its power. Or maybe I was simply in denial. Whatever it was, I shared my secret:

When I was sixteen, the same age as Maria's son, I tried to kill myself. It was around that time in my life when Gary told me everyone would think I was beautiful if only I were white. The time when I couldn't put my finger on why I felt so different and ashamed, so the problem must be me. I must be broken. I'd been lying on my bed and thinking about how I'd never get into an Ivy League school like Zahid had and how disappointed my parents would be. I felt that I was, at my very core, a disappointment to myself too. I just felt stuck. Stuck in a story I didn't like. So, on a Saturday night, I took a bunch of pills and tried to die.

Being a teenager can be so hard, having to operate in that place between childhood and adulthood, with so little real power but with so many driving hungers. I felt so alone, so irredeemably different.

I woke up the next morning as sick as I've ever been.

I could barely lift my head up or see straight. The shooting pains in my stomach were unrelenting. I was dizzy and nauseated and ashamed. Ashamed because I wanted to die and ashamed because it was one more thing I hadn't succeeded at. I spent the next six days oscillating between throwing up and sitting curled up in a ball in the corner of my room. A stomach flu, I told my parents, who called the school to explain my absence and left a plate of dry toast on my bedside table before they went to work every morning. They never knew what really happened.

The only person I told was my friend Lisa, the one who later said, "If we don't like who we are, why would anyone else like us?" Lisa and I had been friends since the third grade. She was white, Jewish, fit in well with the kids at school—all the normal things I wanted to be. Lisa also always accepted me, never made me feel different or less than, and we could tell each other anything. She rushed over when I told her the morning after. She rushed over and just stayed with me. She didn't judge me; she didn't scold me or advise me; she just showed up and hugged me—and then made me laugh with our usual banter. She checked on me every day after school that week. It was because of her, and because of my fear of disappointing my mom and dad, that I recovered. It's not that I was no longer in pain, but I came out the other side knowing how my actions would affect my friends and family. I also had a new focus: to hide what I'd done. I was so ashamed I had tried, and I was so lucky I had failed.

So, I went back to my life as a misfit, as a girl who'd be pretty if only she were white, carrying this secret. Things changed in college, and again after, and again and again and again. I got to have a life, with all its joys and sorrows.

I went into the world, where I got to see that there is an infinity of choices, and that there are all kinds of people, that when I zoom out, everyone is different and weird, and therefore everyone belongs. I figured out that I get to pick my story.

Turns out, you get to pick your story too. You get to decide the words you choose, how you describe yourself and your life. You get to decide to imagine the possibilities. You shape your story. You tell your story. What a relief to finally learn that. If only Maria's son could have known that—but what teenager does? I sometimes wonder, though, if I had been more honest, if I had shared my secret with Maria, with my community, could it have trickled down and made a difference? Could we all make more of a difference by sharing our stories?

Today, several years since May 21, 2018, most of my scars are gone, and I look largely unscathed. I think about those first hours in the emergency room, when my eyes were swollen shut and I felt like, well—like I'd been run over by a car. Three times, with the tires going over me five times. Almost everyone who saw me, who heard the story, repeated the same things:

"It's a miracle."

"You must have been saved for a reason."

"You'll need to pay it forward."

I'm no longer overwhelmed by that responsibility. My body is not the same body I had before the accident. I will probably always have some pain. There are some things I will never be able to do. My mind is not the same mind I had before the accident either. And that's OK.

I've been practicing acceptance for a while now. It's not

a state of mind you reach and say, "Whee! I've accepted myself and all my flaws, and life here on out will be grand." It's often a process of putting the memories and angst aside for a time and then sometimes being woken again to the pain, then repeating the process until you finally accept the situation and move on. It's a gradual act of forgetting and then remembering, forgetting and remembering.

Do I still sometimes wish I could be that pre-accident powerhouse, that beautiful vase? Sure. But more often, I can look at the changes within me and find those golden seams:

Before impact, I managed large teams and engagements, with a hundred and one fires burning at all times. It wasn't just that I handled chaos; it was that I thrived on it. Now, I prefer to focus on a few things at a time and really dig deep.

Before impact, I loved crowded, loud events and meeting new people. Now, I appreciate smaller groups and more-intimate interactions.

Before impact, you could drop me in a brand-new city and I'd happily improvise my way through it. Now, I need a little time to acclimate and settle in before getting down to business.

Before impact, the only fuel I needed was chai lattes, five or six hours of shut-eye, and my husband's motto, "Sleep is for the weak!" Now, I need a good night's sleep and plenty of downtime so I can rest and recharge.

Before impact, I was certain I could think my way out of anything. Now, I've accepted my diagnosis of PTSD and all its ramifications, and that I need help, maybe forever, to manage it.

Before impact, I worried about appearing weak and

kept my personal issues to myself. Now, I am open about my cracks, and I value authenticity and honesty in all my relationships.

Before impact, receiving help stressed me out, and I considered acts of kindness a debt to be repaid. Now, I accept help and appreciate kindness for the gift that it is—for both the giver and the receiver.

Because of a bizarre, terrible accident, I am a stronger, more empathetic person. I have found more ways to connect with the world around me. I get to pay it forward by being a good partner, mother, colleague, and friend. I get to tell a new story, tell you a story, in the hope that maybe we all do.

PART 4
MY SERMON

I postpone death by living, by suffering, by error, by risking, by giving, by losing.

—Anaïs Nin

I shall now step up on my soapbox, for this is my full-on preachy part of the book. I realize that if you're reading this, you've either gotten a little impatient and have skipped to the end of the book because you just want the bottom line on what I learned; or you have read the entire book and are curious how to apply all of this to your own life. Either way, I hope you find sustainable value in these final thoughts. Many of them might seem obvious; however, these ideas and insights have made me stronger and happier. These are the ten things I want to never forget . . . and if I sound sanctimonious as I try to pay it forward, please forgive me!

#1 LOVE BIG AND LOVE OPENLY

When I was underneath the car, certain that I was dying, I talked to myself about how I had lived and what I would leave behind. I decided that I was satisfied with who I was, that I was a good person, a silly and spontaneous person who owned her life.

Plus I'd told my kids I loved them and showed my kids I loved them every day. They didn't need a letter to tell them what they already knew. The letter I wrote—which is still there in the kitchen drawer, possibly unread—ended up being for my own peace of mind. In ink, on paper, I had expressed my thoughts on life; I had expressed who I was, but they knew those things about me without those written words; they knew me and my love for them from our daily life together.

Yet I still felt one deep regret. Many of the people whom I respected and cherished probably didn't know I held them in high esteem. Most relationships aren't like the one I had with my parents, in which there was no doubt how much we loved each other though we never talked about it. Most relationships don't have that luxury of knowing without words, and I wished I had expressed my appreciation more, that the other people I loved and who loved me knew how important they were to me.

In the days after Maria's son's suicide and at his vigil, people shared how much he had touched their lives. He'd helped other kids on the fringes feel like they belonged. He had been so deeply appreciated and loved. I can only hope that he knew that before he died.

Sharing love and giving compliments should be a habit. Let no one wonder how much they mean to you. Even if it's awkward at first, this kind of love gets easier with practice. Anyway, it's worth it. Because wouldn't you rather love big and openly and have no regrets at the end of the line?

#2 PRIORITIZE SHARED MOMENTS

The only thing we have once someone is gone is our memory of our shared moments with them. Had I died on May 21, 2018, then my family and friends would have had many shared moments to remember, many times we'd laughed and eaten ice cream and swum in deep blue waters. I'd said yes to life, to fun. I'd stayed out too late. I'd been present, and so I would live on in those memories.

During the pandemic, when in-person activities were put on hold, it emphasized just how important it is to be present and engaged with those we care about, and that we sometimes need to get a little creative in how we get together. No matter what, when you're there, whether in person or online, be there, sharing the moment. It's that feeling of your presence and attention that people will remember.

This holds true for the people you know and the big adventures you take and the people you just meet and the brief interactions you share. Sometimes just being present ourselves makes the people around us more engaged and more open to sharing and connecting as fellow humans—and that in itself is so desperately important. Remember my soccer sideline moment? Sharing openly with another mom gave me new insights into PTSD. It gave me permission to live and love more openly (see #1 in this section!). It doesn't need to be a magical, joyful moment. It's about connecting with someone else and recognizing our shared humanity in this big, beautiful world.

#3 LET PEOPLE HELP

This was a hard lesson for me to learn. As strange as it may sound, dying under a car would have been much easier for me, a professional powerhouse and supermom, than surviving with grace.

People sympathized, more than I wanted them to. Strangers sent me cards. Friends and acquaintances delivered flowers and meals and offered to drive my kids. People (correctly) thought I needed help, which made me feel weak and a little pathetic. Did people see me as a victim? Yes! I was run over three times! Was being seen that way such a bad thing? Maybe not.

In the beginning, I really sucked at accepting help. Fortunately, I had no choice but to learn that I wasn't weak, that accepting help is an act of kindness and courage. Pretending that you don't need help just makes everything harder. Letting people support you with gestures big or small gives them a sense of control in a difficult situation and allows them to heal with you. Remember my hairstylist, and how her mom didn't accept any help during her battle with cancer? That still hurt her years later. Accepting help is not just for you; it's for everyone.

By the way, I think this insight also helped my marriage. As a pre-accident powerhouse who could juggle it all, I didn't give my husband enough credit or opportunity to be my true partner. I would just "do everything" and then accuse him of "not doing anything"—but what could he do if I had already done it? When he had the chance to help, when I was forced to let him, he surprised me with his nurturing, his multitasking, and his strength to keep me and our life afloat.

 SAY "SORRY"

The driver never apologized or showed any remorse. Not the day she hit me, when Westcott said, "Don't you care what happened to her?" Not the day I saw her at traffic court. Not two years later in the attorney's office. Each failure to show basic kindness sent me into a tailspin.

To me, that lack of remorse was a crime far worse than hitting me. Mistakes happen—that's life. However, not saying "sorry" is inexcusable. Not saying "sorry" makes the wounds so much harder to heal.

Most mistakes aren't as obvious as running over someone with a car.

But whenever you hurt someone, intentionally or not, you have the power to own it. The power to understand where the other person is coming from, and the role you played in the interaction. You can try to understand the context. Try to look at the person with compassion.

Then, remember the lesson from Life 101: Say you're sorry. It really can be as simple as that for someone to move forward.

#5 DON'T ASK; JUST TELL

Guess what? Questions are hard when you are in a crisis. Especially in the first days and weeks after the accident, a simple "How are you?" would send me into a tailspin.

How am I? I'd think. Where do I even begin, especially when I don't have the strength to even stand?

Even well-intentioned questions can be a lot of work when your brain isn't functioning fully or you are in the middle of a crisis.

I appreciated the outpouring of love and support from my community, but questions were very complicated at the time. For months after the accident, I couldn't bear to listen to voice mails, afraid of what those well-intentioned messages might require of me. I wanted to be sincere but didn't want to be a downer, a fine line to walk when your nervous system is already overloaded. I worried about what the questioner really wanted to hear and whether an honest answer would cause them stress or anguish.

Now, when someone is in a complex situation and I want to show support, I just say, "Thinking about you. If I can help with anything, let me know." Avoiding questions doesn't mean avoiding the person. Show you care in other ways, knowing that answering thoughtful, heartfelt questions really might be too much.

#6 CELEBRATE YOUR CRACKS

It's OK for you to be broken. It's OK to not be perfect. Not everything has to be beautiful.

Kintsugi ("golden mending") is the Japanese art of rejoining broken pottery, not with glue, to try and make it look perfect and never broken, but with gold-infused lacquer, to highlight and thereby celebrate the cracks rather than trying to hide them. I practiced this art by lining my scars with gold glitter in those early days of recovery. I adopted its philosophy in recognizing that our broken pieces, our cracks and scars, make us stronger and more beautiful. Your journey makes you who you are. The seams left by your unique brokenness make you beautiful. Plus when you show your cracks, share your battles, you can also share your victories. The people who accept you for all the imperfections deserve to bask in your sunshine too.

Once I let myself embrace the cracks, I was able to enjoy the new, changed me. The accident is an integral part of me, and, strangely enough, I feel lucky for having had the experience. Appreciating my journey also gave me the strength to write this book, to be this vulnerable, to believe in myself as having something to offer to people like you (and wow, you're reading my book—thank you!).

#7 BE VULNERABLE AND CONNECT

Once I began to embrace being vulnerable, sharing my cracks, and accepting help, I slowed down and realized just how much I didn't know about many of the people around me. It's true that we don't often take the time to go below the surface. As I began to open up, people opened up right back. Through casual conversations with just a little bit of extra honesty, I learned of personal struggles, defining moments, and amazing accomplishments. I got to know wonderful people, many of whom I had known for years, and finally built closer, more satisfying relationships with them.

Surprisingly, it didn't take much work to reach these deeper, more intimate, and rewarding relationships. I discovered that people want to connect. Someone just needs to take the first step in being vulnerable, giving a little more than normal, and then accepting with kindness, gratitude, and without judgment. Why shouldn't that someone be you?

#8 SOMETIMES WE CAN'T JUST THINK OUR WAY OUT OF IT

The revelation that post-traumatic stress disorder is not just mental—that it's physical too—was such a gift to my recovery. In my mind, I had been weak for not having gotten "over" the accident. I knew I had physical issues; I accepted that I still needed medications to regulate my anxiety, but I also *couldn't* accept that. I so badly wanted my mental strength to fix my "mental" issues. I wanted to simply be strong enough, self-sufficient enough to handle it all.

I'd lived most of my adult life thinking through problems and solving them. I'd found success both personally and professionally, and I thought I had the secret. I fought so hard to keep living this way after the accident, to think through the pain, to tough it out. I went back to my teenage brain, thinking there was something fundamentally wrong with me. Why couldn't I just cross the street with my kids? Why couldn't I jump back into work faster? I had to learn the other side of mental toughness—vulnerability.

By finally understanding that PTSD was psychological, physical, and physiological, I was able to accept that I wasn't weak or weak minded. I learned that I needed to pay attention to the signals of my body and to retrain my physical impulses just as much as I needed to work on having a good attitude. We really can't think our way out of everything, and that's OK.

#9 IT'S NOT ALWAYS PERSONAL

Remember #4, saying "I'm sorry"? One thing that I continue to struggle to accept is the driver's lack of remorse or regard for me as a fellow human being. It makes no sense to me, and I have a hard time accepting it. The only way I can move on is remembering that we are all going through some stuff. Just like a traumatic brain injury or PTSD, our struggles aren't always visible, but they are real. While the driver's actions certainly—drastically—changed my life, it was not personal. When I finally recognized this, I was able to let go of some of my pain and disappointment.

And remember those people who said the pedestrian must have been "distracted," and that's why they were hit? Well, they didn't know who I was. They also didn't have any details of what had happened. Yet they needed to protect themselves—and to believe *they* would be safe walking across the street because they wouldn't be distracted. It's a self-defense mechanism.

Here's something else: There were a few individuals whom I was very close to, who pulled back from me after the accident. They went from being very regular, some even daily, parts of my life to almost completely absent. A dear friend and close colleague was one of them.

I couldn't understand or imagine a reason why he, or any close friend, would be so distant during such a tumultuous period in my life until I understood that my trauma may have opened old wounds for him. For some people, I was now a trigger. Had I understood that earlier, I might have been able to sidestep a lot of disappointment, knowing that it wasn't a failure of friendship—it was just the natural instinct to keep out of harm's way.

We don't always find out why someone disappears from our lives, and that not knowing can be really hard. Remember that every person is a universe, with so much going on that has nothing to do with you. They may come back to you; they may not—either way, it's not always about you. Maybe sometimes we just need to enjoy the moments we had and accept that the relationship has evolved, just like we have.

A few of the people I dedicated this book to fall into this category. I ruminated on including them and ultimately decided not to let the evolution keep me from recognizing the impact they made in my life. I'm grateful for their friendship, even if our shared time together has ended.

#10  BE NET POSITIVE

For me, the most impactful lesson was probably the simplest. It takes me back to high school physics: We, and all objects, react to the energy around us. We react to our parents, kids, friends, colleagues, random people of the world, just as they react to us. We are driven by and drive that energy. So, let's make it net positive.

We can do so in a multitude of ways—in our voices, our body language, what we share with each other, how we talk about our days, how we approach our roles and responsibilities. Net positive does not mean we ignore the tough stuff; not every problem can be fixed with high fives, big smiles, and inspirational quotes. It means we bring more positive than negative. We dig deep into our empathy; we work to collaborate; we strive to connect; and we do what we can to leave people with more optimism than skepticism. We bring love, and human compassion, to every moment . . . and paying it forward is probably the easiest way to be net positive.

When the nurses told me it was a miracle I survived, that I was saved for a reason, that I needed to pay it forward, I was too overwhelmed to imagine how I ever could. My life was shattered. Pay it forward? I had nothing left.

What I have since discovered is that paying it forward doesn't cost much. By giving of yourself, by sharing your story, your struggles, your triumphs, your Unbreakable Day—or Days—you give others permission to tell theirs too. The story you tell yourself and those around you has the power to transform fear and shame into compassion and hope. Those stories can remind you that you are not just broken; they can remind you that you can't have the strength of golden seams if you were never beautifully cracked.

EPILOGUE

My Unbreakable Day is May 21. Every year, I celebrate one of the worst moments of my life and its aftermath, and how it brought me to this moment.

I was lucky in that I went into my accident having thought about who I wanted to be when a crisis struck. I knew I wanted to come out stronger. However, thinking that was easy; doing it was much harder. Somehow, though, I did—we did it. We made it through.

We all have cracks. Parts of our journey that weren't easy, that may at one point make us feel ugly or less than, and yet those moments are now part of us, and we have the power to learn from them. Appreciate them.

You also have, or will have, your own Unbreakable Day. Whether it's a specific event or an actual day on the calendar doesn't matter. If you've survived long enough to read this book, then you've been through some stuff. Illness, injury, loss. Rejection and failure and disappointment. But here you are, cracks and all. Maybe you didn't go into it knowing who you wanted to be when you came out of it— yet you came out of it, and you probably learned a thing or two. Recognize that. Appreciate it. Even celebrate it.

Your Unbreakable Day is the moment, the event, the long journey during which your life changed. You changed. It's the day or days or undesignated stretch of time that marks the choice you made to celebrate being alive and staying alive. It's the moment you decided to write your own story. It does not mean we pretend the really horrible stuff wasn't painful, horrific, devastating. It just means we thank ourselves for making it through, and we thank those who helped us get there.

I am so grateful to everyone who has helped me pick up the pieces and carried me through the complexities of this terrible, magical accident. I am so grateful to you, the reader, whoever you are, wherever you are. I wish you a happy Unbreakable Day.

Figure 2. Police assessing how to lift the car off me. (Photo taken by Westcott)

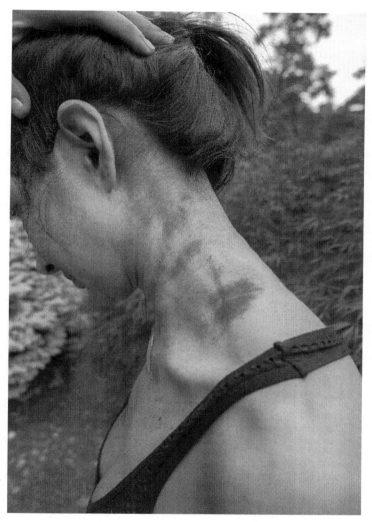

Figure 3. Tire-mark bruising a week after the car ran over my head and neck. (Photo taken by Yasmeen Anderson)

ACKNOWLEDGMENTS

There are so many people I want to thank for making this book a reality.

Thank you, Westcott. Thank you for keeping our life running in the toughest of moments and for the unconditional support as I wrote this book. Your calm keeps me and my crazy in check, and I couldn't conquer the world without you. Thanks, hon.

Thank you, Ashakiran, Jasper, and Kalyan, for the joy and love you bring to my life every day. Thank you for making me feel like a superhero for surviving and for all the props you gave me as I wrote this book. You have cheered me on, helped make my "in the zone writing" moments better by bringing me a fluffy animal, a sparkling water, or a decadent chocolate snack. You even offered your college fund to help me self-publish. You are the best. My joie de vivre. Thank you for filling my bucket every single day.

Thank you, Bret Hanson, Bobby Solomon, and Carolyn Disbrow, for reading my early drafts and encouraging me to keep writing. You made this book a reality. If it weren't for your confidence in me and your belief that this was a worthwhile story to tell, I probably never would have made it to the finish line.

Thank you, Zahid. You have not only given me a lifetime

of wisdom; you have helped me find the value and joy in being a misfit. Thank you for always coming to my rescue and for being my brilliant misfit role model.

Thank you, Robin and Ethan. We are so lucky to have you as our dearest friends. You have been our family and our rocks since we met fifteen years ago. Thank you for taking care of us in our time of need and for the many wonderful evenings and excursions over the years.

Thank you, Lisa, for always accepting me as I am and for showing up every time I have needed you. Whenever I hear your voice, it still feels like we are kids; third grade can't really be almost forty years ago!

Thank you, Mom and Dad. I hope somehow, somewhere, you know that I am writing this book, and I really hope you like it! Thank you for being stylish, fabulous people and generous, loving parents. I miss you and love you both so much.

Thank you, Maria. You have been a source of strength, wisdom, and laughter since we met twenty-five years ago. You are the sister I always wanted, and it's wonderful to know I can tell you anything and you will still love me in the morning!

Thank you, Girl Friday Productions—you are such a wonderful group to work with! Christina, thanks for all the support and coaching as I started the journey, and an extra-special thanks to Mari and Georgie, who held my hand through this publishing process. You have all been delightful to work with, and I may need to write another book just so we can work together again!

Thank you, Anna Katz, for helping me formulate my words and figure out what was—and wasn't—interesting!

Thank you, Miriam Hathaway, for the great edits and beautiful comments you left throughout the manuscript.

Thank you, Janice Chen, for reading my first full draft and sharing your thoughts chapter by chapter—and for being open enough to tell me that you didn't think you would like it but you actually really did! Love your honesty!

Thank you to my team of doctors, Dr. Sofia Shapiro, Dr. Gregory Rauscher, Dr. William Oppenheim; to my therapist, Linda Ditullio; and to my legal team at Brach Eichler: you all helped me navigate daunting waters in the days and weeks after the accident—and even today. Thank you.

Thank you, Yasmeen Anderson, for capturing the tire marks on my neck (my favorite accident picture) and for capturing me for the cover of this book. You make everything look beautiful.

Thank you to the very cuddly ones who always make me smile—Chachi, Ollie, Karma, Gizmo, Sammy, and Coco.

Thank you, Parvez and Suruchi. Your amazing enthusiasm and encouragement felt like the joyful, ecstatic reaction my dad would have had for the book. Thank you. I am so lucky to call you family—and neighbors!

Finally, thank you to so many amazing people in my life. Whether or not our paths still cross often, you have played a special part in my life and in shaping this story. Thank you, Allison, Amy, Anjum, Bart, Bayo, Boo, Carlos, David, Donny, Eddie, Fred, Greg, Hillary, Hitha, Jenny, Karen, Michelle, Mishell, Noelle, Rebecca, Shey, Simon, Stacey, and Tasneem . . . and many wonderful friends and colleagues at Microsoft and Google (hopefully you know who you are).

. . . and THANK YOU to anyone reading this book. I really
hope you enjoyed it!

. . . and PS—thank you to a few other people, characters,
books, paintings, and songs that I want to acknowledge as
never-ending inspiration and sources of joy:

> Howard Roark in *The Fountainhead* by Ayn Rand
> Sabina in *The Unbearable Lightness of Being* by
> Milan Kundera
> Daniel Craig as James Bond
> *Separation* by Edvard Munch
> The Mark Rothko Room at the Tate Modern
> Anna Wintour and the beautiful pages of *Vogue*
> "Lovely Day" by Bill Withers
> "Roman Holiday" by Halsey

ABOUT THE AUTHOR

Naseem Rochette is a seasoned sales leader, working mother, occasional wedding officiant, and passionate speaker on trauma, transformation, and the value of celebrating both victories and struggles.

She has more than twenty years of experience across early-stage start-ups as well as established companies, including Google, Microsoft, and Ernst & Young.

In Naseem's ongoing effort to understand and interpret the world, she has earned a master's in journalism from Columbia University and an MBA from Rutgers University, where she was a founding member of the Rutgers Design Thinking Advisory Board. She also has a bachelor's in English literature from the University of Maryland and an executive certificate in organizational leadership from Rollins College.

At home in South Orange, New Jersey, Naseem enjoys her very own menagerie, including three children, four cats, two dogs, and one husband—a bundle of chaos and joy she calls her personal youth serum.

Throughout Naseem's life, career, and academic adventures, she has taken pride in her ability to help people solve problems, ideate possibilities, and foster trust and collaboration among diverse teams. However, it wasn't until her near-death moment that she found her real courage and most impactful gift: the strength to appreciate—and share—the imperfections and insights that inspire transformation in all of us.

Made in the USA
Middletown, DE
11 August 2023

36478085R00106